Praise for *Preaching to Those Walking Away*

"For decades now, Graham Standish has been inviting Christian leaders to defect from nostalgia (looking back to some golden age) and join him in creative engagement, moving from old, settled assumptions, through a transformation process of unlearning and letting go, to a new journey. In *Preaching to Those Walking Away*, Standish shares what he has learned (and continues to learn) about preaching. I would wish this book on every seminarian, preacher, and teacher everywhere. Intelligent, passionate, clear, and practical . . . it's just the guidance we need right now."

—Brian D. McLaren, author of *Faith after Doubt*

"In an age when people are leaving church and not coming back, preachers need all the help they can get. Thankfully, Graham Standish has brought his deep wisdom and experience to bear on the topic of preaching, and the result is a thoughtful, accessible book that will transform the way preachers think about their art. For a long time now, Standish has been one of our most trusted guides in pointing the way toward spiritual renewal in congregations—and he's done it again!"

—L. Roger Owens, professor of Christian spirituality and ministry, Pittsburgh Theological Seminary

"Standish calls contemporary preachers to a transformational, postmodern, apostolic proclamation for the sake of the nones and dones. He delivers a compelling and inspirational argument for preaching to those who have been and are still walking away from a church that does not speak to them."

—Laura L. H. Barbins, bishop, Northeastern Ohio Synod, Evangelical Lutheran Church in America

"*Preaching to Those Walking Away* is the right book for this historic moment. Every preacher who longs for greater impact needs to dive into this inspirational, practical book. Graham Standish provides fresh ideas drawn from many perspectives, with artful sermon illustrations sure to inspire."

—Lori Carrell, chancellor, University of Minnesota Rochester, and author of *Preaching That Matters: Reflective Practices for Transforming Sermons* (Rowman & Littlefield, 2013) and *Communicate for a Change: Revitalizing Conversations for Higher Education* (Johns Hopkins University Press, 2021)

"In our current environment, there is a lot of hand-wringing about the decline in church attendance but not a lot of willingness to change our practices to meet those who are going or already gone. Graham Standish provides clear, practical recommendations on how the preacher might speak to the hearts of those who are seeking spiritual nurture and not finding it in church. A worthy read."

—Kym Lucas, bishop, Episcopal Church in Colorado

"As churches seek to adapt to an ever-changing world, they need new frameworks, not just more information. *Preaching to Those Walking Away* provides a new and compelling vision for preaching to a modern world, one that looks dramatically different from the one most clergy were trained to engage. Thought-provoking and well-considered, Standish's latest book is an important read for anyone concerned about the future of the church."

—Josh Packard, executive director, Springtide Research Institute, and coauthor of *Stuck: Why Clergy Are Alienated from Their Calling, Congregation, and Career . . . and What to Do about It*

PREACHING TO THOSE WALKING AWAY

PREACHING
TO THOSE
WALKING
AWAY

N. Graham Standish

FORTRESS PRESS

MINNEAPOLIS

PREACHING TO THOSE WALKING AWAY

Cover design: Laurie Ingram Art + Design
Cover image: MJgraphics/Shutterstock

Print ISBN: 978-1-5064-7171-6
eBook ISBN: 978-1-5064-7172-3

*To all the pastors I am fortunate to serve as a guide and friend for.
You have formed me deeply in more ways than you'll ever know!*

Contents

Acknowledgments

Looking back on my career as a pastor and now as a spiritual guide and coach for pastors (in addition to running a counseling center), one thing stands out: *I just don't think the way others do.* I was trained in seminary to think like a pastor, but I've also been trained to think like a therapist, spiritual director, coach, teacher, and nonprofit leader. Having studied deeply in the fields of organizational psychology and development, cognitive behavioral psychology, addictions, psychodynamic psychology, generational theory, the philosophy of science, comparative religion, mythology, marketing, communications theory, and more, I now think in those ways too. I've never felt compelled to prioritize one field over the other but instead have always felt called to integrate them in unique ways. Unfortunately, pastoral ministry often struggles to be integrative. We're not sure we like new ways of thinking.

Integrating a myriad of perspectives has made me a different kind of pastor. A friend the other day, upon reading Adam Grant's wonderful book *Think Again: The Power of Knowing What You Don't Know*, said to me, "Standish! I now get you. You're like what Grant says. You refuse to let science take a back seat. You think about faith scientifically, always testing assumptions." In modern American life, having someone say that to you normally sounds wonderful and leads one to think, "Yes, I am unique! I am an individual!" My thought was, "Yeah, that's why I've always felt alone."

People who think differently in the church usually aren't rewarded. They're criticized. I have been criticized, but so what? Even more, I've been deeply blessed because while I've sometimes *felt* alone, I've never actually *been* alone. So many people have supported me in my calling and drive to integrate these diverse fields into ministry. It's important to share with you who these people are because they have been a blessing to me and keep people from being alone.

I want to thank my wife, Diane, who has patiently (well, most of the time) listened to me vent and dream as I've tried to figure out how all of my experiences and ideas fit together. Also thank you to my dear friends in ministry, Ralph Lowe and Connie Frierson, who have valued me and my approach to ministry, making it much easier to think differently.

I want to thank the board of Samaritan Counseling, Guidance, Consulting, where I now serve as executive director, for valuing my writing and permitting me to make it part of my position. Also thank you to the members of Samaritan's Caring for Clergy and Congregations Committee, the Reverends Melissa Stoller, Sarah Robbins, Susan Rothenberg, and Tim Black, who have helped me grow our program to reach out and care for pastors and churches. I especially want to thank our leadership team for Samaritan—Susan Young, Luci Ramsey, and Beth Healey—for their support of my writing but even more for training me ever more deeply in the labyrinthine world of leading a counseling center. It's been an amazing education and a deep, underlying part of this book. It's a privilege to lead an organization devoted so deeply to being Samaritans—to being people who notice the hidden wounds of others and fearlessly tend to their deeper personal wounds.

I will always be deeply grateful for Calvin Presbyterian Church in Zelienople, Pennsylvania, where I was senior pastor for twenty-two years, and especially for my successor, the Reverend David Paul. Both the church and David have been incredibly supportive of me even though I've been away for four years.

Also, I so deeply appreciate the members of the Leadership Renewal Group of Presbyterian pastors whom I facilitate in thinking differently. This is a group of pastors who study the thinking and writings from many different perspectives outside of the church and then vie together to integrate these ideas into their ministries. It is so much fun to be part of a small community of pastors seeking more and discovering how their ministries are growing and becoming fruitful as they do.

I want to thank my editor for this book, Beth Gaede, who has worked with me now on five of my last six books. She is an incredible editor, pushing me to clarify when necessary, pushing back against me when warranted, and generally helping me become a better writer each time. Even more, she's a friend.

Finally, thank you! This is my sixth book on transforming leadership and congregations. For whatever reason, I've felt called to help pastors and churches overcome the massive decline taking place in the mainline church. These books have explored grounding the church in discernment and prayer, crafting a humble approach to leadership, transforming worship, developing simple rules for healthy ministry, and overcoming resistance while encouraging growth. This book has been a passion of mine for years because it addresses something I've struggled with since I initially felt called to ministry: how to reach out to people walking away from church, people like myself. The fact that you are reading this means you share some of my passion for this. I am so appreciative that you are considering taking this up. So thank you!

INTRODUCTION

I have a confession to make about my preaching. Actually, it's about my training to become a preacher. I've shared this confession with very few people over the years, mainly because it invites criticism from colleagues. Here it is: I skipped most of my homiletic classes in seminary.

Laypeople understand my reasons more than pastors do. They've sat through enough aloof, abstract, disorganized, and disconnected sermons to understand my reasons for doing so. Pastors tend to be less forgiving: How can you skip the training for the most essential part of our calling?

Why would someone preparing to be a preacher skip most of the classes preparing her or him to be a preacher? The answer is simple: I didn't want to be trained by *them*—by those training me in the accepted, traditional ways. I aspired to something more. I can be quite stubborn in my principles, but this was more than that and more than believing that I didn't need to be taught how to preach. I knew that I needed to be trained. I just didn't want traditional, main-line church training.

Let me try to explain as best I can why I didn't want to be taught traditional homiletical sermon making, and remember that I'm referring to training from the mid-1980s, not necessarily now. The simplest explanation is that I struggled to pay attention through the first three classes and then thought to myself, "These are the most boring classes I've ever been in." I decided then and there that I didn't want to learn bad preaching habits from my professors. My objection was not just that a class this tedious, droning, and overly intellectual would reflect the kind of preaching I would be taught but that it would perpetuate in me the kind of preaching I had walked away from in ninth grade.

This leads to the longer explanation, which goes deeper and begins with my leaving church at age fifteen to join the ranks of the growing "spiritual but not religious" movement. I grew up in the 1970s during a time when it seemed like every pastor preached in a way that I've come to call "preaching from the book of platitudes." The sermons were mostly formulaic. They typically offered intellectual, dispassionate treatises on . . . I never listened long enough to know what they really were about.

When there was passion in the sermon, it was often pointing out human sin. I still remember the Presbyterian pastor of my late childhood and early adolescence preaching from a pulpit set eight feet above the floor, looking down at us over his half-moon reading glasses, telling us something along the lines of, "We are all worms! We don't deserve God's love, but God is merciful despite our evil. We are sinners of the worst kind! Grace is our only salvation." Oh, my. It's a wonder anyone would return after a sermon like that. I already felt bad enough as a kid who constantly got into trouble. Why go to church and listen to someone tell me that I could look forward to a life where no matter what I did, I was probably facing an eternity of God-given detention?

Oh, yeah, he did dangle in front of us the possibility of receiving grace and mercy from that angry God, but I wondered, What happens when grace runs out? What happens if God decides I'm not worthy to receive this gift of grace? If that's the case, I'm screwed! Suffice to say, if I hadn't been forced to go to church, I would have left it years earlier than I did.

I felt virtually nothing inspiring or spiritual in those sermons. They were judgments. They were chastising punishments, and they were boring to boot. They felt theologically full and spiritually empty. I just wasn't some teenage malcontent, too immature to realize the profundity of his sermons. I actually had deep spiritual yearnings. I had experienced God many times in my young life—while climbing a tree as a child and sensing God's awareness of me, while standing at the communion rail of an Episcopal church as the priest placed his hand on my head and said a prayer of blessing, in prayer during dark times that I don't need to go into here. I wasn't looking to rebel. I was looking to embrace. I wanted to experience God, and the experience of being told that I'm nothing more than just a dirty worm was not opening me up to an experience of God's presence and love.

One pastor did keep me from completely disregarding all preaching. During my confirmation class year, the judgy pastor was replaced by the Reverend George Wirth, whose preaching was much more positive and engaging. Unfortunately, his style of preaching came too late to prevent me from joining the ranks of the spiritual but not religious.

Searching for "Something More"

Like many who proclaimed themselves to be on a spiritual search outside of the church, I dabbled in a lot of different spiritual perspectives (hold on to that thought, because what we do with different spiritual perspectives will come up in the ensuing chapters). I did this for nine years, rarely crossing the threshold of a church until a personal crisis led me back a mere eight months before entering seminary.

I didn't go to seminary to become a pastor. I went to become a better therapist. (I enrolled in a joint program with the University of Pittsburgh where I could simultaneously get a master of social work.) I wanted to learn how to deal with spiritual issues that came up during counseling—with the "something more" that people with spiritual struggles often yearn for. Prior to that I had been a child and adolescent therapist in a psychiatric hospital and had counseled a number of teens who had spiritual issues. One patient had hallucinations of Jesus appearing in a window that helped him heal. Another had a schizophrenic breakdown and repetitively chanted about Jesus while locked in a secure room meant to keep him safe. Several others were dabbling in satanic worship while listening to a steady diet of heavy metal music. Others had attempted suicide and wondered aloud where God was in all of their struggles. And yes, I was still searching spiritually. I eventually joined a church, but I was still skeptical. I was still "spiritual but not religious," and I felt as though I was always just a few missteps from walking away again.

This brings us back to my homiletics classes. To their credit, the profs weren't teaching me how to preach like the crabby pastor of my youth. But the style of preaching they were teaching still felt like it was rooted in spiritual neglect. I was yearning to preach to people like me who had walked away from church in their search for God. Instead, I was about to be trained in preaching to someone who had been calcified in the pew since 1933. For example, we were told to study the writing style of Eudora Welty, the famous Southern author known for her exquisite, detailed literary descriptions in her novels and short stories. We were told to pay attention to her focus on detail. Absolutely nothing wrong with paying attention to details in our stories, as you'll see later when we talk about how to make our sermons sticky. The problem was that preaching is an oral form of communication rather than a literary one. Sermons that have exquisite *literary* detail are also sermons that entice daydreaming, fidgeting, napping, and drooling. I am totally willing to read pages of exquisite detail, but listening to them is different because our brains aren't built for literary listening (we'll talk more about brain structure and preaching later), unless we're listening to an absolutely great voice in an audiobook. There's a reason publishers employ great actors to narrate them.

They're Searching for Experience, Not Explanation

I recognized that we were being taught to essentially "preach our papers in public." Sermons were treated as though they were miniacademic treatises that were *said* rather than *read*, and who wants to listen to a long, academic treatise? We were required to do exegetical examinations of Scripture (translated from the original Greek or Hebrew, if possible) as we studied academic commentaries exploring the history, context, authors, and audiences of the passages we used as our homiletical foundations. We were then supposed to explicate the theology embedded in the passages. Stories were encouraged, but they were there only to explicate the theology. The sermons we were being taught to craft were complex, intellectual, aloof, and scholarly. Why? Because we were being shaped through academic institutions by those who prized academic study. They were training us to preach to parishioners like *them* rather than to those who were attending our churches (or increasingly *not* attending our churches). They were definitely not showing us how to preach to those who had walked away.

At this point, you may be starting to feel defensively protective of a more traditional approach and training. Don't be. Remember that my question is, How do we preach to people who are always on the verge of walking away? Much of my career as a pastor has been focused on how to preach to people who have walked away from the mainline church and aren't interested in evangelical, nondenominational preaching. I wanted to reach the spiritual but not religious. I wanted to reach people who would become "dones" (done with church but not with God) and "nones" (have no belief in God and increasingly see religion as a weakness).

I struggled with how I was about to be taught to preach because I intuitively knew it was a style that could never reach someone like me. Not only would it not reach my fifteen-year-old self, but it wasn't reaching me at age twenty-four. So after the first two classes, I stopped going. Out of the remaining eight classes, I showed up for maybe four of them so that I wouldn't be docked for lack of attendance, but I left halfway through three of them. I wasn't being obstinate or stubborn. Nor was I lazy. I just didn't want to be taught how to preach to those who were already there. I wanted to learn how to preach to people like me—a person who was yearning for something deeper, more spiritual, and more energizing.

Again, let me stop here for a moment, because I sense you may be tempted to draw pistols at dawn in order to defend the honor of theology. Don't. I'm not attacking theology, although I am questioning the dominance of theological thinking and preaching in the mainline church when those walking away aren't yearning for theological answers. There's a reason people proclaim themselves to be *spiritual* but not religious and then satisfy their spiritual yearnings by reading Eckhart Tolle, attending weekly yoga classes, streaming videos of Deepak Chopra, and even following Gwyneth Paltrow's strange spiritual musings and buying her increasingly weird Goop products. When they say they are spiritual but not religious, they are telling us two things.

First, they are telling us that we are *religious* but not spiritual, and in many cases, they are right. In the mainline church, we've emphasized for centuries staid religious ritual over spiritual experience. In fact, in the mainline church, we're generally skeptical of spiritual experiences if they happen outside of our beloved liturgy or traditionally acceptable forms, such as Scripture reading, reflection, or contemplation. These people are seeking spiritual *experience*. They may not be seeking a Pentecostal experience, but they are seeking an encounter with the Divine, the Holy, the Transcendent—with God. Lofty, abstract, religious sermons don't speak to their spiritual struggle. For example, on Easter, they're neither yearning to hear how they've been forgiven for all their sins by Jesus dying on the cross, seeking rational proof that Jesus was resurrected, nor hoping for an explanation of atonement. They want to know how, if Jesus really exists and is with us, we can find him, experience him, be guided by him, and have our lives made better by him. They want to know where he is in the midst of their illness, divorce, or unemployment or even just amid their existential angst over the course of their lives. They aren't looking for religious, theological answers. They are looking for something spiritual that connects with their deeper questions.

Even more, the younger generations (we'll explore this more later) are grappling with how to band together to overcome climate change, racism, inequality, and division. Again, they aren't looking for lofty, religious sermons abstractly exploring these topics. They want to know how they can tangibly and pragmatically engage in efforts that make a difference. They want to hear preaching that is authentic, honest, compassionate, and unifying—preaching that connects the spiritual with the communal, which ultimately leads to efforts that heal individuals, communities, and the world.

Second, they are not walking around proclaiming themselves to be "*theological* but not religious." In my career as a pastor, I have had hundreds tell me that they visited and became members of our church because they began to experience God through our worship and programs. Never once did anyone tell me that she or he joined because she or he was hungry for Presbyterian or Reformed theology. Never once did anyone say, "I was searching for the right theology, and I found it here." I've rarely heard anyone say, "I became a Lutheran/Episcopalian/Catholic/Baptist because they have the right theology."

Usually when I have spoken with someone seeking a particular brand of theology, I've discovered she or he was a purist looking for the *one* place that satisfied her or his dogmatic search for orthodox truth—a truth that this person was the sole arbiter of. More often, I have heard people say they became whatever they became because they experienced God mentally and even physically in that place, and especially through the sermons. What I've heard consistently is, "It was amazing. It felt as though Pastor So-and-So was speaking directly to me."

Balancing Bones, Body, and Breath

So what's the relationship between the theology we've been trained in and the spirituality that I'm writing about? What role does religious practice play in all of that? I've come to realize that theology, religion, and spirituality are a trinity. Lose one and you weaken the others. I see the three as being like the bones, body, and breath of a living being. Theology is the bones that offer a skeletal foundation for the living body. Almost all creatures have some sort of skeleton, whether it's an endoskeleton or exoskeleton. Whatever it is, it creates a structure. Theology structures religion and spirituality with teachings and concepts that can form a foundation that leads us to experience God and become active in serving God. But we can't live by bones alone.

Religion is the body. It is the physical engagement with the world. It offers ritual, prayer, community, ministry, mission—practices and disciplines that shape the spiritual life. Religious life is a physically and relationally engaging life. A healthy religion has a solid theological foundation and spiritual aliveness, but religion is made for us; we aren't made for religion. Religion gives tangible shape to our theology and spirituality.

Finally, spirituality is the breath. Without breath, we die. We hear how essential breath is in the beginning of the Bible: "Then the Lord God formed man from the dust of the ground, and breathed into his nostrils the breath of life; and the man became a living being" (Gen 2:7). This breath of life is not only for people but for congregations. It is the breath that gave humans life in the garden of Eden, and it's the breath that gave the church life on Pentecost.

Spirituality and religion without a solid theology become like a breathing body with no bones. There's no structure. There's no foundation. It's a blob that takes the shape of . . . whatever. It's like the New Age movement, where anything can be believed and people morph into whatever religious shape their passions lead them toward. It may be a yoga class. It may be a retreat center. It may be candles and crystals. None of those are bad, but they're kind of a blob that never really nurtures a vibrant, diverse community.

Theology and spirituality without religious practice become like wind whistling through a bare skeleton. There's no body. There's no real engagement with the world. It's fragile. We reduce faith to an intellectual assent—believing in the *right* theology, the *right* dogma, the *right* orthodoxy—that becomes almost completely disconnected from experience and the transcendent. It spawns a restricted spirituality based on "beliefs righteousness"—the idea that we are saved by the purity of our beliefs, theology, or orthodoxy. If those beliefs crumble because of crisis or questioning, so does the person's spirit. It can very quickly become rational agnosticism or atheism.

Then there's theology and religion without spirituality, which is where much of the mainline church either is or is heading. That's bones and a body without breath. It's a corpse, which aligns very much with what people are saying about mainline denominations—that we're dead or dying.

The mainline church has been dominated by theological thinking and religious practice that ignore or diminish the spiritual, and it is causing people to walk away. Most of our denominations came of age during the eighteenth and nineteenth centuries' Age of Enlightenment, which emphasized rational thinking over all other modes of perception. This is why the mainline church is guilty of overemphasizing the essentiality of theological thinking over spiritual experience. It's why almost all of our seminaries are titled "Such-and-Such *Theological* Seminary." It's also why people are walking away. We're no longer living in a rationalistic era, trying to explain everything in a sequential, logical, systematic way. We're living in an era of multiple perspectives and ways of knowing that don't always follow logical rules of deduction, trying to reach out to people in search of irrational-seeming experience rather than rational belief.

Who Are Our Models?

So let's return to my seminary experience. I walked away from my homiletics classes not because I thought I knew better. Instead, I walked away because I wanted to learn from those who were reaching the spiritual but not religious, those who today are reaching the dones and the nones. Who were they? I was paying attention to a wide variety of influential speakers. I certainly paid attention to the nondenominational, evangelical preachers of the time who were reaching some while also pushing away many others who were turned off by their more rigid theology and restrictive teachings. I was also paying attention to writers and speakers who mixed psychology and spirituality (such as Wayne Dyer), quantum physics and spirituality (such as Fritjof Capra), medicine and spirituality (such as Andrew Weil), recovery and spirituality (such as John Bradshaw), and more.

Instead of attending homiletic classes, I intentionally studied in depth how evangelical preachers, speakers on PBS specials, well-known authors, and others were reaching the spiritual but not religious. I would watch them on television, notebook in hand, studying their mannerisms, speech patterns, storytelling, and content. I didn't want to become them. I wanted to use what they did to share a Christian message that invited people to become part of a spiritually alive religious congregation that helped transform their lives. I wanted to learn how to encourage people to become spiritual *and* religious.

Since then I've spent my career studying those who teach and preach to those walking away. In more recent years I've studied TED Talks. I've studied YouTube videos. I've studied those who are best at leading people into an authentic transformation of life, regardless of their perspective. This is what I want to invite you also to explore through this book. Many people in our culture have become spiritual preachers for our age, and they aren't in our congregations. I want us to be aware of—and integrate—the valid insights that they share and that we may need to pay attention to.

I consider what you are about to read not competition for what you may have been—or are being—taught in preaching and homiletics classes. I consider it an expansion of what you've learned and are learning. Over the years, I've read very good books on preaching and have watched "great" preachers preach. But even our great preachers are reaching fewer people. Why? Because they and we hold on to styles that no longer work—standing behind obstructive pulpits, reading off carefully worded manuscripts, using stylized preaching voices, speaking to people's intellects rather than their whole person, speaking to what we think they should know rather than to the questions they are struggling with, and prioritizing intellect over experience.

So this book is intentional about *not* exploring ideas coming out of the Christian homiletical world and instead exploring ideas that come from other fields that are impacting modern communication. It shares the insights I've gained over the years from studying the postmodern era (we'll explore this in chapter 3), generational theory (chapter 4), multiple intelligences theory (chapter 5), neuroscience, communications and marketing (chapter 6), TED Talk principles, spirituality, group therapy, narrative theory, and more (sprinkled through all of the chapters). My hope is that as you read this, you will discover ways of preaching that begin to feel more dynamic and powerful to you and your congregation and that transform lives while also maintaining a sense of authenticity. My hope is that it will challenge you to consider how to preach to those who are increasingly walking away from our churches. If we don't start preaching in a way that reaches them, we will find many of our churches gone in the not too distant future, replaced by movements that are willing to stretch, grow, and reach people in new ways.

CHAPTER 1

THE PROBLEM OF
PRESENT-DAY PREACHING

It was November 1991. I was a young associate pastor taking part in an interdenominational Thanksgiving Eve worship service at a nearby Methodist church. We were a collection of solo and senior pastors and me. I may have been part of this congress of clergy, but I was the insignificant one because of my youth and position. I was assigned the role typically offered to associate pastors in ministerial gatherings—look humble, look holy, and keep my short prayer after communion *very* short. I was literally given the "least of these."

An older pastor, who definitely looked the part of a pastor with gravitas, gave the sermon. I don't remember much of what he said, but I clearly remember how he said it. Speaking in a shaky vibrato voice, he said, "We are here todaaaaaaaaaaaaayyyyyyyy to be graaaaaaaaaaate- fuuuuuuuul for everything Jeeeeeeeesuuuuuus has given ussssssssssssss." It's impossible to capture in writing how strange his voice was. It quivered as though he was constantly on the verge of tears, which made me study his face to determine if those were tears on his cheeks or just light reflecting through his bifocals.

My immature, snarky mind kept wondering, "Where'd that voice come from? Does he talk with his wife like that over dinner? Does he really think it helps people listen better?" His voice was exactly like one of those old-time preachers I'd heard in recordings of radio programs from the Great Depression. Why would he want to sound like a 1930s radio preacher in 1991?

Ignoring his words but transfixed by his voice, I had a sudden insight: this guy's preaching in the wrong era. He was preaching for people long since dead. That led to another insight: What if we're all preaching to the wrong era? What if *all our* styles of peaching are thirty or more years behind? I've been wondering about this ever since, but it's become more of an observation rather than a question. We're all preaching for a bygone era. We're all at least thirty years behind.

His voice and style actually got in the way of his message. Was his message one that might have made a difference in my life? Who knows? I was so caught up in his odd intonations that I have no idea what he was preaching. His style obscured a deeper message. In fact, his problem is shared by many people with searing and potentially transforming insights. If the manner of the message doesn't resonate with the listeners, then the message will never be given a chance. Having studied at the master and doctoral level, I have been transformed by some of the greatest thinkers alive, but it took a lot of work for me to get there because some of them are the worst writers alive. I've had to work to be available to their transforming insights. Unfortunately, those listening to our sermons rarely are willing to work that hard. If our style of preaching doesn't resonate, our insights will be ignored. The important point is this: *preaching is meant to transform lives, but if our style of preaching doesn't resonate with the audience, it will have little transforming power, even if the foundational message is the greatest one of all time.*

A millennial pastor recently validated this particular insight to me. I was leading a workshop, "Preaching to Those Walking Away," which is the foundation for much of what I'm writing about in this book. During the second workshop, he said, "Graham, I realize now what my frustration as a preacher has been since I was ordained. In seminary, I was taught by baby boomer professors how to preach to baby boomers. You're giving me permission to be a millennial preaching to millennials." I *was* giving him permission—permission to preach to people of the era we're in.

I had the chance a number of years ago to explore my insights about transforming worship for the present era in my book *In God's Presence*.[1] In that book, I explored how worship has constantly undergone transformation since the beginning of Christianity, noting how church leaders within each historical era crafted a different kind of worship experience precisely for its era. The art of preaching has similarly undergone a constant transformation. Delivering a sermon as part of worship has remained foundational, but the style of preaching—the *veneer* we laminate it with—has undergone constant transformation.

Whether we're talking about furniture, siding, bathrooms, or kitchens, veneers change over time. We remodel all of them because personal tastes and styles change, and we have to update them for the age we're in. Kitchen remodeling comes to mind as a metaphor because my wife and I remodeled our kitchen less than six months ago. When it was finally done, we were both amazed, in retrospect, at how outdated, inefficient, and shoddy our previous, comfortable kitchen had been. We kept commenting, "My gosh, we should have done this ten years ago!"

The struggle of preaching in the present era is similar to remodeling a kitchen. We become so comfortable with previous preaching styles that we don't realize how outdated and inadequate they've become. The old pastor's preaching during the Thanksgiving Eve service was like stepping into a kitchen from the 1930s—it was jarring how outdated it was. It was foundationally still a sermon, but the structural and vocal veneers were from a bygone era.

The problem for modern preachers, the reason we are preaching to eras that have passed away, is that we constantly confuse cherished preaching *veneers* with the preaching *foundation*. What's the difference? The foundation of preaching is the exploration and explanation of Scripture in a way that helps people live lives aware of, open to, and in pursuit of God's presence and guidance. That is the *why* of preaching, its purpose, and that purpose never changes, no matter what form our preaching takes.

How we preach, though, has changed through the ages. The style of preaching we use now is different from the style used by Jesus, Peter, Paul, the early Christians, the church fathers, or anyone from the first few centuries of Christianity. If we could transport them to the twenty-first century as guest preachers for this Sunday, we'd witness most of our church members zoning out, checking their phones, or falling asleep fairly quickly. Why? Because the early Christian style of preaching, honed during an age when people focused and listened better, wouldn't work in an age of distracted thinking and multitasking. Their preaching had a *veneer* designed for their times. That veneer felt authentic in those times. Now they'd feel out of touch. In the same way, if we were transported to their times, our style would baffle them (assuming we could speak Aramaic fluently).

So what exactly is a veneer? It's something created in a style conforming to a particular age or era that we affix or laminate onto a foundational support. It's a style of flooring or furniture covering or siding that engages the senses of those living at that time. Anyone who has bought a house or moved into a new apartment understands. There's always something we have to update to suit us, even if it's just a new coat of paint.

Preaching veneers are the customary or contemporary forms of preaching we use to teach and preach the gospel. It is the structure of the sermon we employ (three-point? plot-based? four-page? twenty-minute?), where and how we stand, the kind of voice we use, whether we use a manuscript or outline, the facial and physical gestures we use, and more. A veneer reflects the cultural preferences of a particular age, and just as kitchen styles are always changing, preaching veneers change constantly over time too, forcing us to adapt or watch our congregations decline. The reality is that adapting over time is hard (for some it feels impossible), yet if we don't adapt, younger generations will gravitate toward those who have. So what do we change to? The answer isn't necessarily to adopt a completely new style that isn't you—that wouldn't work any better than your grandparents suddenly decorating their living room in a hip-hop style to make them seem more "hip" to their grandkids. The veneer we use is important, but it has to still be authentic to who we are.

Despite my having just said that our preaching has to be authentic to who we are, veneers are never truly authentic—at least not in an eternal way. They always reflect the personal tastes of a particular age or population. What matters is the foundation—its frame and its function. If the framing is good and allows it to function properly, then we can adapt our veneer to meet changing tastes. If the foundation is rotting underneath and it no longer truly serves its purpose, then nothing affixed to it can last. At its foundations, preaching is transformational. Its framing is a worship service designed to help people experience and encounter God. Its function is to open us to God's guidance so that we can live wiser, more compassionate, more aware, and more consonant lives. Simply put, preaching opens us to God's presence and calling. As long as that's the foundation, we can then develop a preaching veneer, a preaching style that helps listeners feel both at home and ready to listen and learn. The veneer is what makes what we offer attractive, but the foundations are what transform listeners. The two are deeply intertwined, and one doesn't work without the other. Still, only one changes over time. The function doesn't, but much like an oven used to cook food, the style does. And the updated styles tend to be more effective in doing what it was foundationally built for.

A Short History of Preaching

Using the historical schema I employed for *In God's Presence*,[2] I want to trace the different veneers of preaching that have been employed throughout the ages. This is not intended as a scholarly look at the history of preaching. Instead, I'm going to explore both how preaching has evolved over two millennia and how adapting to each era has been a significant factor in Christianity's growth. What's allowed Christianity to endure has been how Christians across the ages have adapted their preaching veneers to new eras and even new cultures (I'm not going to explore the cultural aspect here), even if those adaptations have been painful for those who've loved the previous ones. Or, as I sometimes have kidded to a congregation while preaching, "Ah, those were the good old days, when sermons lasted two hours and people stayed awake." The following sections trace preaching styles from Jesus to today.

Preaching in the Early Church

It's hard to know exactly how the first Christian pastors preached, since it's only the rare sermons that have been preserved, but we do get inklings of what early preaching may have been like by looking in both the Gospels and the book of Acts. In the Gospels, we quickly discover a style of preaching that was grounded in Scripture but utilized practical metaphors and personal testimony. For instance, Jesus used parables culled from farming, shepherding, and village experiences. Still, it's hard to extrapolate from the Gospels exactly how Jesus preached, since they don't quite present one style of preaching. Matthew's, Mark's, and Luke's Gospels portray Jesus's sermons as being either direct, simple teachings or metaphorical parables. In contrast, John's Gospel portrays Jesus as presenting deeper, more complex teachings with few metaphors.

If I were to guess which versions were more authentic, I would suggest Jesus employed two different styles and adapted them to his audiences. To the crowds, he offered those direct, parable-based sermons, while with his disciples-in-training and followers, he offered sermons and lessons that were more deeply spiritual and that stretched them theologically.

Peering into Acts, we get a bit more evidence of the early church preaching style. For example, Peter offers a sermon at the beginning of Acts that is fairly Jewish in style:

Men of Judea and all who live in Jerusalem, let this be known to you, and listen to what I say. Indeed, these are not drunk, as you suppose, for it is only nine o'clock in the morning. No, this is what was spoken through the prophet Joel:

"In the last days it will be, God declares,
that I will pour out my Spirit upon all flesh,
    and your sons and your daughters shall prophesy,
and your young men shall see visions,
    and your old men shall dream dreams.

19

Even upon my slaves, both men and women,
    in those days I will pour out my Spirit;
        and they shall prophesy.
And I will show portents in the heaven above
    and signs on the earth below,
        blood, and fire, and smoky mist.
The sun shall be turned to darkness
    and the moon to blood,
        before the coming of the Lord's great and glorious day.
Then everyone who calls on the name of the Lord shall be saved."
    (Acts 2:14b–21)

Afterward, Peter makes his biblical and theological case that Jesus was the fruition of Scripture. His sermon's style would have felt familiar to his Jewish listeners, as he speaks to what they just witnessed, cites Scripture they are familiar with, and then tells them what is happening now and how it's the fruition of prophecies they'd been raised with. It's a pretty straightforward explication of biblical history and prophecy. It gives an indication that Jewish rabbinical preaching may have been more of an intellectual explication of Scripture than what we might find in modern preaching.

Later in Acts, we see how quickly preaching adopted a nuanced veneer. Paul preaches atop the Areopagus—Mars Hill, the traditional place for philosophers and thinkers to present new ideas to the people of Athens. That sermon is very different from Peter's on Pentecost, and it isn't necessarily because Paul is a different preacher. Paul knew he was preaching to those steeped in Greek philosophy rather than Hebrew Scripture. He offers no appeals to Genesis or Exodus nor to the words of the prophets or the history of the Jews. Paul preaches as a Greek philosopher might:

Athenians, I see how extremely religious you are in every way. For as I went through the city and looked carefully at the objects of your worship, I found among them an altar with the inscription, "To an unknown god." What therefore you worship as unknown, this I proclaim to you. The God who made the world and everything in it, he who is Lord of heaven and earth, does not live in shrines made by human hands, nor is he served by human hands, as though he needed anything, since he himself gives to all mortals life and breath and all things. From one ancestor he made all nations to inhabit the whole earth, and he allotted the times of their existence and the boundaries of the places where they would live, so that they would search for God and perhaps grope for him and find him—though indeed he is not far from each one of us. For "In him we live and move and have our being"; as even some of your own poets have said, "For we too are his offspring." (Acts 17:22–28)

Paul and Peter each knew who they were preaching to and adapted their sermons to those gathered. As the early churches formed, preaching quickly integrated the scriptural approach of the Jews with the philosophical approach of the Greeks and Romans. They were foreshadowing how preaching developed over the next two centuries as preaching synthesized Jewish Scripture with Greek logic. When reading the preserved sermons of the church fathers, we see that they increasingly wrote and made arguments that corresponded with a Greek philosophical style, appealing as much to reason as to Scripture.

Ultimately, any dive into the preaching of Jesus and the apostles brings us face-to-face with a significant problem: their sermons in the Bible aren't their real sermons. They are summaries of sermons by the authors of the Gospels and Acts. For example, I doubt that

Jesus actually preached what we've come to know as the Sermon on the Mount. I seriously doubt that he preached in that bap-bap-bap manner, jumping from topic to topic—a style much more suited to slow and reflective reading than straining to listen to a man some distance away. Imagine listening to a sermon like the Sermon on the Mount on a Sunday morning. Sure, you'd be OK reading it in your den afterward, but would you have been able to pay full attention to it as it jumped quickly from topic to topic? Matthew's Sermon on the Mount is a literary device used to share Jesus's greatest hits in one sermon. It's like a medley of an artist's top hits. It employs a literary veneer to best communicate the messages Matthew and others might have heard in any number of sermons by Jesus.

What makes it even less likely to have been an actual sermon is that in those days, no one would have followed Jesus around—parchment, reed, and ink in hand—scribbling down his sermons. The same would have been true for the apostles' sermons in Acts. The sermons we've received are summaries shared by the Gospel writers. Still, we get glimpses of the early church's styles as they adapted to both Jewish and Greco-Roman listeners.

From these biblical beginnings, preaching styles adapted slowly, although asserting this is a bit fraught because I'm approaching it from a Greco-Roman historical perspective. I willingly admit that I have no idea what preaching looked like when the apostle Thomas (according to the oral tradition of his life beyond the Gospels) brought Christianity first to the Indus River Valley in what is now Pakistan and then onto what is now India. I would imagine he adapted his preaching to these cultures. The same can probably be said of Andrew, who according to tradition, preached around the Black Sea, went up the Dnieper River (where it's said that he prophesied about the eventual founding of Kyiv), and perhaps went as far north as Novgorod in what is now Russia, near its border with Estonia.

22

With all of this in mind, for its first three hundred years, the early church followed the model of the Jewish synagogue, which became the dominant place for worship in both Judaism and Christianity after the destruction of the temple in Jerusalem in 70 CE. The synagogue movement was rooted in the tradition of the Pharisees, while temple worship was rooted in the Sadducee tradition. Christian communities adapted the synagogue for the gentile population, forming what were essentially house churches. Early Christians typically worshipped either in people's homes or in homelike buildings designated as small churches. These were intimate services where preaching was more instructional and an outgrowth of the study of Scripture.

Again, not having troves of house church sermons on hand to study, it's hard to completely know what the preaching was like, but we can extrapolate from what is available. The Mennonite historian Alan Kreider explored what he calls the improbable, exponential growth of Christianity in the Roman Empire during the first few centuries of persecution. He says that early Christian preaching did not evangelically appeal to the Great Commission (Matt 28:19–20) or try to answer great theological questions (although early Christian preachers did teach doctrinal topics such as the Trinity and baptism).[3]

Kreider speculates that the worship services—and by extension the preaching—emphasized pragmatic living. It emphasized their *habitus*, their way of living as Christians: "It was not Christian worship that attracted outsiders; it was Christians who attracted them, and outsiders found the Christians attractive because of their Christian habitus, which catechesis and worship had formed."[4]

The preaching would have been much more didactic, offering teachings on how to live according to Christ's way, using Scripture as a foundation, which leads to the development of life habits that include patience, charity, compassion, honesty, and more. One thing to remember is that the early Christians were mostly illiterate, so sermons and teachings had to be simple in order to help people grasp profound ideas through the telling of biblical and Christian stories, sharing simple Christian biblical teachings, and discussing how to live these out. The teachings were most likely built upon Scripture passages that the early Christians memorized prior to their baptism, chief among them being the Sermon on the Mount.[5] In fact, the Sermon on the Mount played a significant part in the formation of early Christians prior to the acceptance of the Apostles' Creed in the early church. Imagine what Christian life might look like today if instead of memorizing and reciting a statement of what we believe (the Apostles' Creed), we had members memorize and recite how we are to live (the Sermon on the Mount).

What's important for this discussion is that for the early church's first three hundred years, Christians became very adept at preaching to those who were walking away, although these listeners were walking away from other faiths to become Christian, despite the danger of potential persecution and imprisonment. There was something about the early Christians, formed through the worship, teaching, and preaching of the early church, that allowed them to adapt to their neighbors' various cultures. They didn't just adapt to the Greco-Roman world. They adapted to the many, many cultures both within and beyond the Roman Empire.

This last point is important to the central idea of this book—that transformative preaching is built on a solid foundation yet is able to adopt veneers from the surrounding culture and in harmony with that particular era that help people undergo spiritual and life transformation. If, as you'll see in later chapters, our preaching isn't transformative, it is not foundational. At any rate, there was most likely quite a bit of diversity of preaching in the early church. As Christianity spread to so many places, it had to adapt to its new environments.

Preaching in the Established Church

When Constantine first decriminalized Christianity in 313 CE and then declared it the religion of the state in 380 CE through the Edict of Thessalonica, Christian preaching underwent a significant transformation. At first the preaching was in Latin or Greek, because those were the languages of the Roman Empire. Over time, especially as portions of the Western Roman Empire were increasingly conquered and degraded by northern tribes such as the Goths, Visigoths, Vandals, Lombards, and others, the common language changed. The leaders of these conquering tribes often converted to Christianity, but not because of compelling preaching. Rather, they recognized that if they became "Christian" rulers, they could more easily subdue their conquered subjects. In part because these invaders were not schooled in Latin, that language fell out of use, becoming merely the language of the church. Consequently, preaching became more inaccessible and somewhat mysterious—or at least mysterious to those who lacked Latin education. For the ensuing thousand years, the preaching of the dominant Roman Catholic and Eastern Orthodox traditions became less and less about instructing the people and more and more about instructing the religious elite—priests, monks, bishops, and those with higher education.

Eventually, this latinized and ritualized form of Christianity morphed into what I call "preaching sideways." Instead of facing the congregation and preaching to them, the preachers (speaking entirely in Latin) would preach to the religious seated in the chancel across from them. Over time, rood screens (wooden structures obscuring a full view of the chancel) were constructed in the churches, which further separated the laity from the elite religious. The common people were reduced to being witnesses of the priests preaching in a mysterious language to the holy elite. Preaching became something the laity endured, much like

25

the Eucharist, which also was reserved for the religious elite. The priest would stand before the congregation and hold the elements aloft while the laity passed by genuflecting or remonstrating. Afterward, the religious elite would share communion with each other.

These Christian laity weren't instructed by the sermons. Their instruction came from the extravagant art displayed in medieval churches. Laity, bored from watching priests babble on in Latin, could look around the sanctuary and see carved statues, reliefs, and stained glass windows that taught them the Christian stories. They saw crucifixes and Madonnas, symbols of Eden and creation, tablets symbolizing the Ten Commandments, and depictions of David versus Goliath, Solomon on his throne, the apostles in symbolic attire, and the apocalypse. They were being preached to through art, which also meant that they didn't have much exposure to the prophets or the Epistles, since it's really difficult to carve a statue that reflects Isaiah or Romans or James. The advent of the Renaissance, and eventually the Reformation, changed this style of preaching, and it became more laity focused.

Preaching in the Literary Era

As the pursuit of new ideas and knowledge exploded during the Renaissance and its aftermath, more and more laity became at least somewhat educated. They began to read the Bible for themselves, albeit in Latin at first. Eventually, the crusade to translate the Bible into everyday languages gained momentum. We tend to think of the Reformation, beginning with Martin Luther's nailing of his Ninety-Five Theses to the Wittenberg Church door, as the advent of laity reading Scripture for themselves in their own languages. In reality, the Roman Catholic Church had been fighting against this movement for at least one hundred years prior to that. We can imagine why the church, which had ceased preaching to the laity centuries before, would consider as dangerous and heretical the translation of the Bible and the subsequent preaching to laity in their own language. With the advent of the Reformation, the floodgates were opened as the Protestant movements grew throughout Europe. Eventually, during the Counter-Reformation, even the Roman Catholic Church allowed preaching in the common tongue to resume, with a focus on educating the laity.

Through this movement, preaching became more literary in style. Sermons became like academic treatises that often lasted two hours or more as the preachers laid out their biblical and theological cases. Protestant preachers became less like priests presiding over a sacrifice and more like academic scholars instructing a class. In fact, my tradition, the Presbyterian tradition, maintains a remnant of this era. Presbyterian pastors in worship are typically garbed in black academic robes. If the pastor has a doctoral degree, she or he will bear three stripes on each sleeve of the robe, indicating that the pastor has this level of education. These aren't liturgical robes. These academic robes are indistinguishable from those worn by college professors on graduation day or by Harry Potter and his friends at Hogwarts.

As more laity were trained to read and listen to increasingly academic speaking and writing, the sermons became much like what I call "preaching our papers in public." Much of modern, mainline preaching maintains this approach, even if we no longer get to preach those great, two-hour sermons (those really were the good old days, weren't they?). It is the remnants of this era that cause pastors of the modern, mainline church to struggle to adapt to those walking away. Most mainline pastors are still trained in an academic style reminiscent of the sixteenth century. Also, preaching increasingly focused on both the prophets and the Epistles. The apostle Paul went from being the forgotten man during the era of art and stained glass to the prominent man, beginning with Martin Luther, who based much of his Ninety-Five Theses on insights gleaned from Paul's Epistle to the Romans. Literary preaching lasted another four hundred years until an invention that significantly changed preaching.

Preaching in the Oral Era

The invention of the radio significantly changed preaching in ways that some pastors still struggle to adapt to almost one hundred years later. The seeds of this change really began one hundred years prior with the tent preachers of the various Great Awakenings, as preaching was modified to appeal to more rural, less educated Christians. Preaching through broadcast radio, building upon the tent-preaching style, became more colloquial and direct as preachers addressed the laity's concerns, whether they be about salvation, marriage, parenting, or socioreligious norms and mores. Radio broadcast speeches, stories, and dramas into people's living rooms. Preachers worked on making sermons easier for listeners to understand. Sermons became shorter to appeal to shrinking attention spans. This style was in stark contrast to that of previous ages, where congregants were trained either to listen to long, academic sermons or to stand quietly while watching priests speak mysteriously in Latin to each other.

With the advent of radio, the emphasis became more and more on enticing people to listen. Thus, their attention was drawn to the character and quality of the preacher's voice. Remember the story I told at the beginning about the old pastor preaching at the Thanksgiving Eve service, whose voice sounded as though he was preaching to people in the 1930s? He was trained in the style, the veneer, of the oral era. It was all about his voice, and his voice was shaky with elongated vowels because that's what the radio preachers of his youth sounded like. Go online and listen to preaching from the 1930s through the 1950s. Their voices have strange lilts and twirls and were modulated to captivate. If you do listen, you will find yourself fascinated for at least a little while, perhaps wondering how someone developed that kind of voice and whether "he" used that voice at the dinner table or a party. It was completely manufactured to attain and retain listeners. In fact, it was cultivated because of the limitations of early microphone technology and the need to modulate the voice to maintain listeners.[6]

Preaching in the Visual Era

Most of us modern, mainline preachers have been raised during the visual era. This era began in earnest in the 1950s and 1960s with the growth of television. Just as in the 1930s and 1940s, when radio became established in people's homes, during this era, most people bought televisions. Increasingly what mattered was how pastors looked, their gestures, and their physical presence. In the late 1950s and early 1960s, well-dressed and well-coiffed preachers appeared more and more on television.

For example, in the Roman Catholic Church, we saw the rise of Bishop Fulton Sheen, who established himself first in the oral era with a dynamic vocal presentation and then migrated to television, where people were captured by his compelling looks—thin build, striking eyes, authoritative yet calm demeanor, and regal vestments. The evangelical equivalent of Bishop Sheen was Billy Graham, who similarly started in radio and migrated to television, preaching with dramatic voice and gestures and dressed in a well-styled suit. Graham's ministry gave rise to a generation of televangelists such as Jimmy Swaggart, Jerry Falwell Sr., Rex Humbard, Ernest Angley, Kathryn Kuhlman, and more, who had all honed their styles both on radio and in live presentations.

Preaching in this era has emphasized how to capture people's ears *and* eyes. Preaching has moved out of the pulpit and onto the floor, so preachers can effectively use gestures to emphasize important points. This era recognizes that how we look is almost as important as what we say. This doesn't mean that preachers have to look "good." It simply means that preachers started cultivating looks that were distinctive. The medium becomes the message. It's a difficult era for those who don't want to be judged by how they look. Still, it's a reality. In the visual era, what matters to people isn't just the content of our sermons, as it was in the literary era, nor about whether we can captivate listeners with our voices. Now visuals matter. Sermons throughout this era have become shorter and shorter, or if they haven't, they've been punctuated through the use of background or foreground visuals—projected screens, the use of images or video clips, and the like—to keep our attention. Compelling preachers in this age also maintain eye contact with the congregation as much as possible to create a personal and emotional connection. We can still see the influence of visual preaching in how some younger preachers present themselves: wearing clergy shirts with cut-off sleeves to show off tattoos, sporting "radical" hairstyles, wearing T-shirts with religious messaging, or cultivating a style of dress popular among younger people.

The mainline church has struggled to adapt to this age because of both our tradition and our training. Many mainline preachers still insist on preaching from a manuscript, which violates the rules of the visual era in several ways that encourage people to tune out and walk away:

1. *Manuscript preaching forces the preacher to look down, not up.* This is a pretty obvious observation, but it's more significant than it seems, because generations have grown up watching videos where the stars never fully break eye contact, and even

glances away from the camera are designed to keep us looking. Personal eye contact is important in any conversation or dialogue, yet no matter how well we may preach from a written script, detailed manuscripts force us to look down. Each time we look down for long periods of time, we lose connection with our congregants. At that point, we usually begin to emphasize our voice more than eye contact, thus reverting to an earlier era. So often, when visiting churches, I witness a pastor, scared to look up from a written script, adopting a strange cadence to compensate. Not just older pastors do this; I've seen even young pastors adopt a completely different vocal style from normal speaking when reading Scripture or preaching.

2. *Manuscript preaching is generally academic, not pragmatic.* Most seminary-trained pastors are products of academic training that emphasizes biblical scholarship and theological depth— training that church members have *not* had. They are often unintentionally (and sometimes intentionally) trained to preach to their professors, to craft academic sermons proving intellectual points. Their training makes them good at exploring problems yet poor at offering pragmatic guidance. They intellectualize faith by exploring theological issues yet shy away from offering practical tools for living that we already said the early church excelled at. They are good at theology and poor at spirituality and psychology (a reason that so many of those walking away are increasingly seeking wisdom from therapists rather than pastors).

3. *Manuscript preaching is written to be* read, *not* said. No matter how well we write a manuscript sermon, we use language that is meant to be read. We can't help it. We've not been trained to write dialogue and scripts. Remember, we're trained in academic writing, which means that even when trying to write in

a conversational style, we'll still write sentences without contractions while using idioms of speech we'd never use in a conversation. I call this "Data preaching," after the character Data in *Star Trek: The Next Generation*—an android whose programming does not allow him to use contractions.

4. *Manuscript preaching delivered from behind pulpits feels more like a lecture.* Most mainline pastors are more comfortable standing still behind a pulpit than in front of it. It's a remnant of the literary era when pastors' sermons were academic lectures given from behind a lectern-style pulpit. The struggle is that preaching behind a pulpit is distancing in an era when a sense of personal connection, real or perceived, is valued.

I'm going to return to these ideas again later, even if it's a bit redundant. There's one more era to explore. Over the past twenty years, we have slowly moved out of the visual era into the multimedia era, which really places our standard preaching methods two eras behind if we're reading from manuscripts and modulating our voices.

Preaching in a Multimedia Era

One thing you'll notice about every era since the establishment of the church in the Roman Empire is that each subsequent one has been exponentially shorter than the previous one. While the home-church era lasted for about three hundred years, it was followed by an era that lasted almost one thousand years. That was followed by one that lasted about four hundred years, followed by one that lasted about forty years, followed by one that lasted about thirty years, followed by this one—and who knows how long this one will last before being replaced by another we don't even grasp yet. (Perhaps the postpandemic era will be a mostly virtual one in which in-person worship doesn't matter as much as our online presence and newer technologies and corresponding veneers as yet undeveloped become more prominent.)

The multimedia era has been slowly progressing as the internet age has expanded and the world has shrunk. Sermons in this particular era haven't done away with previous eras. In this era, all aspects of the previous eras are integrated. In a multimedia age, it's not just how we sound and look; postmodern preachers are creating videos that integrate all sorts of special effects, music, images, movie clips, sets and scenes, and so much more. Yet many mainline pastors have been scared of technology and thus have been slow to integrate these new veneers. The Covid-19 pandemic required pastors and churches to adapt by integrating technology despite often strong reluctance and resistance on the part of congregations. The reality is that those pastors and churches that have refused to do so have *increased* their rate of decline as either a new era of pastors and churches attracts those people who no longer resonate with our outdated preaching veneer or those people simply walk away.

The media and the message are intertwined in this kind of preaching. Quirkiness sells, or at least quirky sets and effects can sell. They have adopted new veneers, while we're still tinkering with veneers from the oral and literary eras. Preparing for visual-era sermons could clearly have benefited from drama training as people learned to use their bodies, faces, and voices. In the multimedia era, most pastors would benefit from art school as well as film and drama training. Unfortunately, our lag behind the culture makes it seem as though we're still trying to figure out whether to replace our red flocked wallpaper with striped wallpaper, not realizing that walls are now made of opaque smart-glass windows. To be sure, some people will always be attracted to these fading veneers, but they're part of a shrinking generation.

I apologize for offering an overly blunt message, but those who are walking away are not walking away only from what we say; they're walking away from how we say it. They watch videos on YouTube, TikTok, Instagram, and other platforms that grab their short attention spans, and we're still wondering how to write a well-constructed sermon that would appeal to our parents (or grandparents). What this next generation is seeking is something authentic.

You might be tempted here to dismiss much of the multimedia age as precisely inauthentic because it uses multimedia as a crutch. I'll challenge that. Pastors who preach in a more multimedia way often seem more authentic because, despite their use of special effects and new veneers, they communicate simple messages that can feel spiritually and theologically deep. They know how to captivate others on a simple level in a way that we often don't, using story, personal experiences, humor, sarcasm, absurdity, symbols, and creative metaphors.

What I fear is that younger preachers, who grew up in an era steeped in multimedia, are still being trained to preach in a literary and oral style that doesn't permit them to be fully creative in ways that they already know how to be.

Can We Preach in a More Authentic, Compelling Way?

Those who have walked away from church—who have become nones and dones—are still searching. They haven't quit looking for answers, but they're rejecting the answers provided by mainline church preachers. Part of the problem is the messages we preach. We are preaching from a religion that, no matter how rationally we approach it, is paradoxical and often theologically complex—God is both one and three; Jesus is both fully human and fully divine; we have to lose our lives to save them, become poor if we are to be rich, weak if we are to be strong, and more. Still, people today are searching for authentic voices that speak plainly and compellingly. Do our listeners feel as though we are authentic and compelling in our preaching? Authenticity doesn't mean speaking in a way that's necessarily creative and original. It simply means speaking in a way that *feels* trustworthy, and what's trustworthy to this generation is anything that seems to strip away formal, ceremonious, and aloof veneers. They're a generation that's grown up with manipulative marketing, self-serving leaders, and an older generation that does nothing but hover over them and criticize. So they're skeptical of any kind of social veneers that seem to be hiding an underlying agenda. Unfortunately, we cling to several practices in our preaching that lead younger people to feel as though we are inauthentic. Five questions help us identify them.

1. Are We Stuck behind Pulpits and Lecterns?

I know I spoke about this when talking about manuscript preaching, so this is an extension of that discussion. Where do younger people today experience people talking to them from behind something? Perhaps politicians, who clearly are not trusted much anymore. If you watch TED Talks, you might have noticed that the speakers never stand behind lecterns or tables. They are out front, often using multimedia presentations. Watch a YouTube video. People almost never appear behind anything, unless it's a table that holds their makeup, ingredients for a recipe, or tools for a project. When we stand behind something, we are increasing the sense that we are inauthentic. Young adults have grown up watching *Blue's Clues*, Nick Cannon, *Hannah Montana*, and charismatic teachers, all of whom have made connection a key attribute. Even their college and university professors are unlikely to stand behind a lectern. I just did a completely comprehensive survey of college students . . . in my household. According to my two college-aged daughters, almost none of their professors teach from behind a lectern, and the ones who do are considered boring and a bit out of touch. Do we remain behind pulpits because they help, or are we behind them because we're afraid to step out, leave our scripts behind, and be exposed?

2. Do We Use a Different Voice and Syntax from Normal Ones?

Using odd phrasing; flat tones; and quivering, overly emotional, or clinical voices makes listeners feel as though either they are being manipulated or the speaker is hiding something. Our voices should sound normal because that's what people are used to in communication. We need to use sentences and phrasing intended to be said, not read, which include contractions, common intonations, jargon, and idioms. No matter how well we try to write our sermon, we will always use language that's not conversational—language that would be awkward if talking to someone at a party or in a bar.

When working with students preparing for ministry or with pastors looking to improve their preaching, I often give very simple guidance: if the sentence you write wouldn't sound normal in a restaurant said across a table to a friend, translate it into a sentence that would. In other words, speak conversationally. Which would sound more normal, conversational, and authentic in an Easter sermon, "We are gathered here today to celebrate the resurrection of the risen Lord" or "I'm so excited to be here, feeling that Easter joy!"? I've been known to ask seminary students and pastors to read me their sermons as though we were having a beer together. Spend five minutes doing that with a friend, and you'll see exactly what I mean about the inauthentic language we generally use in our sermons.

3. What's Our Eye Contact and Body Movement Like?

Do we carry ourselves in a way that creates connection? Our eyes, face, and body should be natural and integrate normal posture, hand gestures, facial expressions, and more. Think of how we might talk to someone we like when we're sharing a story at a party or standing at a bar or in an office hallway. Please don't misunderstand me. I'm not advocating that we make everything so deeply casual that people wonder if we're drunk. But I am asking us to reflect seriously on how we communicate. Do we stand, gesture, and talk in a way that comes across as personal and perhaps even a bit intimate? Most pastors don't quite realize that what we say is often not as important as how we say it through our facial expressions and hand gestures. We worry so much about people hearing our words that we spend hours crafting "perfect" sentences. That makes sense when writing a book like this one, where you're focused on my writing rather than on me. Sermons aren't books. And if we preach in a way designed to feel authentically personal, people will trust us and become more open to accepting what we say. They'll work harder to understand a poorly crafted idea offered by a person they trust than they will to accept a well-crafted idea from someone who seems aloof. We may not like this fact, but it is the reason they'll follow a false prophet rather than us.

4. Is Our Sermon Written to Be Read or to Be Said?

I spoke quite a bit about this earlier, but it's so important that I want to explore it just a bit more. Our preaching training has often been academic. Academic writing and speaking are generally cognitive, abstract, dispassionate, and discursive, all of which demand that the listener be highly motivated to appreciate and integrate what we are saying. We can tell if our preaching has become overly academic by paying attention to what matters when we are preparing the sermon. Are we focused on cognitive precision, linguistic rigor, correct concepts, and getting our words right? Or are we concerned about how well our messages will be understood?

I worked with a pastor many years ago who told me that he had to preach from a manuscript because there are times when people mishear him and accuse him of saying something he didn't say. He insisted on preaching from a manuscript in order to defend what he really said. Thus, he risked that he might lose a connection in order to preserve correctness. If you're worried about people criticizing you for saying something you didn't say, I have two suggestions for ways to overcome the problem: (1) preach off notes and write out the sermon afterward (thus creating both an oral and a written version of your sermon), or (2) record the sermon and send a recorded version to your critic. Or you can do what I do—I just don't care that much. If someone mishears me, I tell them what I really said, and if they don't agree, c'est la vie.

For me, the pitfall of preaching to be read rather than spoken was captured succinctly in a sermon I heard a few months ago. I was worshipping in a church where I was teaching a Sunday adult education class. The pastor began her sermon with an engaging story about her experience when she was a first-time parent—the fears, the anxieties, the doubts, the joys. I remember the story well because she told it in authentic, compellingly normal, everyday language as she looked each one of us in the eye. She was really good. At the end of the story, though, she shifted to her manuscript. At that point, I could no longer tell you what she said. I zoned out. Looking around, so did most of the others. A significant part of my forgetting was the manner in which she preached once she was done with the story. Almost immediately after her story, she looked down at her manuscript and said something like, "Indeed, when we face situations like this, our anxieties flow as our confidence ebbs." That's a good sentence to put in a paper or a book or an essay. It's not what we would say to a friend sitting across the table. To that person we might say, "It's amazing how anxious I get, especially since I'm not convinced I'm a good parent."

This leads to another significant issue when constructing a sermon to be said rather than read: to what grade level are we preaching? I had a eureka moment twenty years ago during a discussion with our music and youth director, Bruce Smith. We were talking about why books by evangelicals such as Rick Warren seem so different in format, tone, and language from those of mainline church writers. I mentioned that these books sometimes had drawings or pictures in the margins, more white space, and plenty of subheads. I also noted how much more likely people were to read their books than those from the mainline tradition (shockingly including my books!), even though on average, members of mainline churches tend to have higher levels of education than those in the evangelical churches. In short, the evangelical tradition seems to inspire more religious reading. Why?

Bruce very quickly responded, "That's because they're better at the SMOG test." "The what?" I replied. "The SMOG test. It stands for the scientific measurement of gobbledygook."[7] SMOG, much like the Flesch–Kincaid (or Flesch) readability test,[8] assesses the grade level at which something is written—or more accurately, the grade level that a person needs to have attained in order to comprehend a piece of writing. Created by G. Harry McLaughlin, a communications professor at Syracuse University, the test takes sample lines of text from the beginning, middle, and end of the writing and through a mathematical formula estimates the grade level of the writing.

Bruce and I decided to test the grade levels at which mainline versus evangelical writers write and the grade level of my sermons. We discovered that the evangelical books we sampled were typically written at an eighth-grade level. Most mainline books were written at a college-sophomore level. My sermons were written at about an eleventh- or twelfth-grade level.

If you're like most seminary-trained, mainline pastors, you will look at that discrepancy proudly and say, "Yep, I speak to a more intellectually sophisticated group of people." What I realized, in contrast, was that a significant reason people are walking away from church is that most of them stopped their religious education at a fifth-, sixth-, or seventh-grade level (if they had religious education at all). They may have a college-level understanding of science, business, the humanities, or history, but their religious education is stunted at an elementary level. That's when they stopped attending—or at least investing themselves in—worship, Sunday school, or more. If they're willing to engage, we often preach to them at a theological and religious level they aren't prepared for. The evangelicals understand that they have to translate complex ideas to a simpler educational level, which is certainly why they've tended to grow and the mainline has tended to decline. They shape their messages for an increasingly post-Christian, religiously uneducated audience.

Preaching to less lofty educational levels isn't dumbing down. It's simplifying. For instance, which of the following two sentences will have a more profound impact on people: (1) "Discernment happens when we choose with intention to put aside ego and attend to God's personal guidance" or (2) "If you want to hear God, you need to put aside what you want in order to listen for what God wants"? They say essentially the same thing, but the first one is written at a much more sophisticated level, under the assumption that we're speaking to people who have a bachelor- or master-level academic education. Meanwhile, those we're actually preaching to are struggling to keep up because they may have only an eighth-grade religious education.

It doesn't frustrate me to simplify my sermons to reach a less religiously educated population because I know it's important. I do get frustrated listening to atheists debate Christians over God's existence when they simplify religion. This is a bit of a non sequitur, but too often the debating atheists I see on YouTube or television reveal that they only have a fifth- or sixth-grade understanding of religion, even if they hold a master- or doctoral-level science or philosophy education. So their arguments assume a religion that is much more superstitious—and much less sophisticated—than the one I've embraced. They'll speak about science and rational reasoning in erudite ways and then criticize religion for holding on to beliefs that teens were taught to reject in confirmation class.

Ultimately, a sermon written to be said, not read, speaks at the level of the listeners. To meet them, we're willing to do the hard work of making it more conversational and comprehensible while resisting the urge to criticize the listener for not being more sophisticated. The sermon written to be said cares more about transforming the listener than it does about being sophisticated. Preaching at their level is *not* demeaning to our congregants or dumbing down. It is teaching profound ideas in a way that helps people become transformed. In essence, it is preaching to a church, not a seminary. I've often taught seminary students and pastors to preach to their congregation, not their professors. Professors appreciate sophistication and intellectual insight, as they should, since their job is to go ever deeper intellectually. Congregation members want to know where to find God in their lives and how to live better lives. Those who've walked away want to hear messages that speak to where they are and the real struggles they have, not where we wish them to be.

5. Is Our Sermon Spiritual and Experiential or Theological and Analytical?

I will explore this theme in later chapters, so I won't go too far here other than to plant a seed. The people who have walked away from

41

the modern church often call themselves "spiritual but not religious." With that phrase, they are laying a very heavy criticism on the church. Can you hear it? They are saying, in effect, that we are "religious but not spiritual."

People today are looking for a sense of purpose and meaning, *especially* in this dystopian age of division and confusion. University of Michigan behavioral science professor Victor Strecher has studied the search for meaning and purpose in his book *Life on Purpose*. He talks about the importance of having a strong sense of meaning and purpose throughout our lives. In the aftermath of his daughter's death, he discovered a sense of meaning and purpose that he didn't have before. He says, "As an assistant professor at a university, I started caring less about getting tenure and more about making a difference in the world. Most importantly, I stopped thinking that I'd live forever and started thinking that I'm on this earth for an extraordinarily brief period of time—so I should make the most of it."[9]

In his research and subsequent university course on finding purpose and meaning, he discovered that people are thirsty for a life of meaning and purpose. They want to know both why they are alive and how their lives can make a difference. Preaching needs to speak to that. While there are certainly philosophical and theological aspects of the search for meaning and purpose, it is primarily a spiritual search. It's a search for something beyond words, and the most interesting thing about finding meaning and purpose in life is that often it is discovered not through intellectual reflection but through suffering. Fundamentally *the* message of the Bible is on transforming suffering into meaning and purpose. Every single character goes through some level of suffering and discovers God's presence through it that in turn gives them a deeper sense of meaning and purpose as they serve God. Are we preaching in a way that addresses that search?

For our preaching it's important that we grapple with this question in our personal lives as well as our sermons. Remember that those walking away are saying that they are spiritual but not religious. They are not saying that they are theological but not religious, dogmatic but not religious, or liturgical but not religious. They are telling us what they are searching for. Do we listen?

Recognizing this led us on our church website to address this search in explaining who we were as a congregation. While most churches have a page on their website declaring *what they believe*, we created a page instead that declared *why we believe*, telling visitors that we prize the experience of God over certain beliefs about God. In the process, we attracted a fair number of spiritual but not religious visitors and members.

Conclusion

Ultimately, preaching in a way that reaches nones, dones, and the spiritual but not religious requires that we adapt our preaching much as Christianity has adapted to its surrounding culture since the beginning. From its Jewish roots, it adopted veneers that reflected life in the gentile world, the so-called barbarian world, the Renaissance, the Reformation, and the advent of radio, television, and now the multimedia age.

Adapting to the era we're in now requires our willingness to change how we preach. The irony for many pastors is that they grievously lament that their churches resist changing while they then refuse to change their own manner of preaching to reach those walking away. Just as our congregants are reluctant to give up cherished styles of music, hymns, and liturgy, we're often reluctant to give up cherished ways of preaching that have a withering impact in today's culture.

We hold on to our manuscripts, the backsides of our pulpits, our academic language, and our theological orientation. That's fine if we don't mind preaching to the remnant, but it doesn't reach those who are increasingly walking away, never to return—or at least never to return until we adapt.

CHAPTER 2

ARE WE TRANSFORMING OR MERELY CONFORMING?

I'm going to start off with something controversial—something that may cause you to decide that you've read enough and need to walk away. In the process, I'll probably break a taboo, so I'll ease you into it by making you wait a few pages until I do.

Way back when I was in seminary, we had chapel every day around 10:30 a.m. This was a time for students and professors to lead twenty-five-minute worship services for the whole seminary community. As the first year waxed, I waned when it came to chapel. I slowly stopped going. I knew I was supposed to, but I just couldn't keep attending the services.

Eventually, in my second year, the president of the seminary snagged me while I was walking to class: "Graham, Graham, . . . come over here. I want to talk with you about something. When was the last time you went to chapel?" Busted. I tried to think of an excuse: "I dunno, maybe last week?" That wasn't close to true. "You know that going to chapel is part of your education, right?" he replied. "Yeah, I guess so. I'll start going again," I promised.

I went back a few times but soon reverted to my previous pattern. Yes, yes, I know it was part of my commitment to being part of the seminary community, but I couldn't take it anymore. Every time I went, I heard yet another sermon about what we "Christians" were doing wrong and what we weren't doing right. Sometimes it was that we just weren't passionate enough about social justice and so we weren't doing enough to help the poor and marginalized. It might be that we weren't orthodox enough in our theology. Sometimes it was complaints about the modern church and what's wrong with the world and how we need to go back and make Christianity great again. Other times it was about what's wrong with the younger generations these days. Still other times it was a full-blown attack on the culture, the government, politics, the church, capitalism, communism, or whatever else irked them. They used all sorts of semi-interesting ideas, metaphors, and stories to get their messages across, but in the end, I wasn't inspired by finger-wagging sermons.

The students and professors weren't intentionally wagging their fingers. They were passionate and caring and deeply committed to making a difference in the world. Most have gone on to make a difference. They weren't trying to push people like me away. They were simply doing what they had been trained to do. They were being "prophetic."

In the late 1970s, the wonderful biblical scholar Walter Brueggemann published his seminal work, *The Prophetic Imagination*.[1] The book was influential for all of us in seminary at the time, and it remains influential today for good reason. It's a great book with important things to say. For over forty years, students and pastors have been encouraged by Brueggemann to be prophetic preachers—to call out injustice, to call people back to God's way, and to hold accountable all those who allow the world's brokenness to persist. It influenced me, and I have always paid attention to the need to have a prophetic element in my preaching.

My seminary chapel experiences taught me something else, though—that prophetic preaching over time causes people to feel defensive and thus less likely to be transformed rather than more likely. It's not effective. Whatever truth may be in it, it also tends to push people away today just as much as it did to those listening to the prophets three thousand years ago. From minds and mouths less skilled than Brueggemann's, prophetic preaching turns into a constant refrain: "The nagging will continue until your behavior improves!" I don't know about you, but when I'm criticized over and over again, I become more resistant and obstinate. That's why I stopped going to chapel. Everyone was trying to be prophetic, and it wore me down. I wasn't resistant to change, but the constant nagging made me resistant to voices of change.

Prophetic preaching requires a great level of maturity on the part of the listener, who needs to hear what the prophet is saying, agree, and then change her, his, or their behavior. It requires listening without defensiveness, honest and humble self-reflection, and a deep willingness to change. Such listeners are typically not the people the prophet preaches to. If people were already that mature, would there be a need for prophetic preaching? When have prophets ever preached to audiences that mature? Prophetic preaching often pushes away those most in need of transformation unless it's on a topic they already agree on.

People quickly tire of prophets no matter how absolutely right they may be. I have worked with so many pastors who have complained that they are being criticized for their sermons. They're baffled: "I'm just preaching the Gospel. I'm just telling them what Jesus said." We'll discuss their sermons, and they'll tell me what they said. Eventually, I'll ask a simple question: "Do you feel your sermon was prophetic?" Almost always they'll respond, "Oh, yeah. We're supposed to be prophetic." I'll then follow up with a comment: "So when you preach a prophetic sermon, why does it surprise you when they treat you like a prophet?"

They usually pause when I say that. Most laugh. Some bury their heads in their hands. We then discuss what the prophetic experience is—what Jeremiah and Isaiah and Elijah and all the others experienced. I usually then ask another question: "Why do you think the prophets were always going back to the desert? They went there not only to hear God; they went there to hide from those who wanted to brutalize or kill them. The prophets preached prophetically and were treated prophetically."

I then go on to ask a question that I want you to reflect on: "Do you think the apostles preached prophetically?" When I ask that, pastors usually give me a quizzical look. I normally don't let them respond before I say, "No, they preached *apostolically.*" What's the difference?

Prophetic preaching tells people what is really happening in their world and calls them to listen for God's call to change their ways. Prophetic preaching is often brutally honest, and it can elicit brutal responses. Prophetic preaching is definitely necessary at times, but it is rarely successful. The only real biblical example of prophetic preaching that changed behavior was in the story of Jonah. Ironically, that's a story about what happens when we are called to preach prophetically and we resist the call to do so.

So here's where I break the taboo: *Enough with the prophetic preaching. It's time for apostolic preaching.* For us, as New Testament people, I think our models are found in the book of Acts and the writings of Paul. The apostles were honest in their preaching, but the goal was to *transform through love* rather than *change through criticism.* In other words, their preaching was rooted in establishing relationships that open people up to teachings, and those teachings then open them up to being transformed, which then allows them to transform

48

the culture around them. Such preaching can accomplish what the prophet wants but begins by establishing relationships that make people more open and available to transformation. In other words, when I trust you, I'm much more willing to be transformed by you.

Apostolic Preaching

As an associate pastor in a church, I grappled with the mantle of being not only prophetic but academic and scholarly too. It led to this evaluation for my annual review: "When Graham preaches, no one ever knows what he's talking about." I still get a bit defensive over that, but I think I know what the issue was.

I was trying so hard to be not only prophetic but also everything else. People were lost inside my complex, critical, and sometimes overwhelming sermons. I prepared sermons like I was making soup. I thought had to include every ingredient on my personal menu for a nutritious meal, but I didn't know how much of each to include. So sometimes I added only a few slices of carrots and a whole cup of pepper instead of the number of carrots and the amount of pepper that would truly satisfy.

This confusing style of prophetic/academic/theological preaching changed when I started to study spirituality. I've often said to people that diving deeply into the Christian spiritual tradition was like finally being given water to drink after having my mouth stuffed with peanut butter and saltines. My seminary training gave me substance, but my study of spirituality allowed me to digest and be nourished by it. In my coursework, I was taught a concept that changed my preaching by making it much more apostolic and much less prophetic. So what is apostolic preaching? To me, it can be summed up in several biblical passages. First, from Paul:

For though I am free with respect to all, I have made myself a slave to all, so that I might win more of them. To the Jews I became as a Jew, in order to win Jews. To those under the law I became as one under the law (though I myself am not under the law) so that I might win those under the law. To those outside the law I became as one outside the law (though I am not free from God's law but am under Christ's law) so that I might win those outside the law. To the weak I became weak, so that I might win the weak. I have become all things to all people, that I might by all means save some. I do it all for the sake of the gospel, so that I may share in its blessings. (1 Cor 9:19–23)

Paul is telling us that as he evangelized new communities, he was sensitive to who they were. He didn't waltz into a gentile community speaking like a Hebrew prophet. He didn't march into a Jewish community speaking like a Greek philosopher or gentile oracle. He became one of them so that he could transform them. He was not the prophet speaking the truth and running back to the desert. He was the apostle, the "sent one," living in community with them, working among them as a businessman tentmaker, sharing meals and life with them, and speaking to them in their own language and ways so that he opened them to Christ's presence and the Spirit's work in their midst.

For many of us pastors, trying to be prophetic means chastising our congregants (whether we're overt or covert, they know when they're being chastised). To be apostolic means to understand their habits, their struggles, their resistances, and their conditions and then to speak to them in a way that is both loving and transforming. Often this means starting with their experiences.

Peter offers us an example of preaching rooted in his listeners' experience, which I explored previously. In the very beginning of Acts, after the crowd has all experienced the sending of the Holy Spirit on Pentecost, Peter begins to preach:

> Men of Judea and all who live in Jerusalem, let this be known to you, and listen to what I say. Indeed, these are not drunk, as you suppose, for it is only nine o'clock in the morning. No, this is what was spoken through the prophet Joel:

> "In the last days it will be, God declares,
> that I will pour out my Spirit upon all flesh,
>   and your sons and your daughters shall prophesy,
> and your young men shall see visions,
>   and your old men shall dream dreams.
> Even upon my slaves, both men and women,
>   in those days I will pour out my Spirit;
>   and they shall prophesy.
> And I will show portents in the heaven above
>   and signs on the earth below,
>   blood, and fire, and smoky mist.
> The sun shall be turned to darkness
>   and the moon to blood,
>   before the coming of the Lord's great and glorious day.
> Then everyone who calls on the name of the Lord shall be
>   saved." (Acts 2:14b–21)

Notice what Peter does. He starts with the crowd's experience of watching the apostles and followers of Jesus speak in all languages while a flame flickers above each one's head. He then preaches about what has happened using their own history and Scripture—the prophet Joel. He uses the prophet's words, but he is being apostolic. He speaks to their hopes and dreams of the day when the Messiah will come. He tells them that the day has come. He and the other apostles then baptize three thousand of the throng.

The key here is that his preaching is grounded in experience, not just theology and doctrine. Peter establishes a connection with his listeners, explains their experiences, and encourages them to join him in a life that will lead to more encounters with, and experiences of, the Holy Spirit.

In both Paul's teachings and Peter's example, we find the foundation for transformative, apostolic preaching. Paul portrays it simply: "Do not be conformed to this world, but be transformed by the renewing of your minds, so that you may discern what is the will of God—what is good and acceptable and perfect" (Rom 12:2). What makes apostolic preaching transformative is that instead of just reporting to people what God wants, it invites them to a life in which their minds will be transformatively renewed by actively and intentionally *discerning* God's will. It doesn't tell them what God wants. It invites them to listen for themselves to what God wants.

The Transformation Process

What helped me truly understand this point of view in preaching was Adrian van Kaam, a Dutch Catholic priest, psychologist, and prolific spiritual writer who founded the program in which I studied spiritual formation for over four years. Van Kaam had a unique ability to take some of the most complex ideas and simplify them so that they could become transformative. One of those ideas was his teaching on the transformation process.[2]

Van Kaam believed that people are constantly undergoing a process of transformation that leads to continual reformation. It's a process of going *from* a particular state of being (what he calls "current formation"),

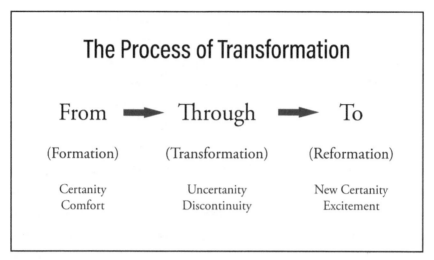

Figure 1.

through a period of transformation, and eventually coming *to* a new, reformed way of living—what he calls "reformation." This ongoing life of transformation and reformation is embraced by those committed to spiritual growth. The Christian spiritual tradition teaches us that an intentional life with Christ is one of constant transformation and reformation, one in which what we were is constantly turning into what we're called to become. In other words, while we are always being transformed in life (at the most basic level, we age), becoming a Christian means being intentional about forming a relationship with God that leads to spiritual transformation. To try to put it in the simplest terms, we choose a life where we say to God, "I'm here. Transform me as you will. Help me become what you want rather than merely what I want." A life of prayer is the path that leads us to a life of Spirit-led transformation. The dead Christian isn't the one who has died but the one who resists growing and being transformed. The Eastern Orthodox tradition has a wonderful way of talking about this call to continual transformation and reformation: *while we were created in God's image, we are called to grow into Christ's likeness.* This is our transformation and reformation in a nutshell.

There's a misunderstanding among many Christians who fear or avoid choosing intentional, ongoing spiritual transformation, opting instead for an immersion in mere theological thinking or religious tradition. They assert that when we become people committed to a life of prayer, we become navel-gazers who embrace an inactive, self-obsessed life as we withdraw from the world. There's a term for people who pursue such a path: *quietism.* Quietism was a movement in the sixteenth and seventeenth centuries of people seeking nothing but prayer. It was also declared a heresy because it turned contemplative prayer into a false idol rather than using contemplative prayer as a vehicle for transformation and action.

A truly prayerful life always leads to transformation and action. Why? Because the person who becomes deeply open to the Spirit is always spurred by the Spirit's call to personal and communal ministry and mission. Deep prayer always leads us, through our intentional discernment, to act in ways of compassion and love that transform people, families, communities, and countries. If you study Christian history, you will discover that the most transforming people—people such as Patrick of Ireland, Augustine of Hippo, Francis of Assisi, Martin Luther, John Calvin, Menno Simons, George Fox, John Wesley, Dorothy Day, Óscar Romero, Mother Teresa, and Martin Luther King Jr.—were all people of deep prayer who heard God's call to action.

As preachers, we invite and lead people through transformation. Figure 1 captures the inherent dynamic of any kind of transforming process—*formation-transformation-reformation*, or *from-through-to*. It all begins with a state of "formation."

As van Kaam would say, at any moment, we reside in a particular state of "formation." We have been "formed" up to that point in a particular way of living that provides a sense of comfort and certainty. I am living in this house, in this town, with this spouse and these children, embracing these values, and holding on to these particular beliefs. Or it could be that I am living in this apartment, with my roommates, perhaps drinking too much at night, while I go to this college and engage in these activities with my friends, living two hours away from my family. Or I might be struggling with an addiction of some sort as I tenuously hold on to my job and my emotionally critical boyfriend. The last one may not seem to be a state of comfort or even one of certainty, but it is. Comfort and certainty don't always mean "happy." What makes it comfortable and certain is the fact that we know what our daily routine is, what pains and traumas our addiction will relieve, or the loneliness that this unhealthy boyfriend lessens. It may not be satisfying and soothing, but there is some comfort in the tenuous stability and familiarity of it all.

The struggle of human life is that we can never hold on to that *one* form forever. We can try, but *transformation is always taking place.* If nothing else, it is ongoing at a cellular level—we're all slowly getting older. We resist change and transformation, but it comes for us anyway. Preachers confront people's resistance to change every Sunday in our sermons. People who come to worship may say that they want to be transformed, but the reality is that they want to be comforted. They would really like to hear a message that says, "You are OK as you are. You don't need to change because you already have the right beliefs about God, you give the right amount of money to the church, and you go to enough meetings to merit God's 'Attaboy!'"

Despite their desire for constancy, when people come to worship, they come to be transformed, even if they're ambivalent about it or resistant to it. Transformation leads us *through* a process that shreds our comfort and certainty. Think of the beginning of any basic transforming experience—your first day at a new school, a first date, the first day on a job, the first day after being furloughed from a job, the moment you realize that your life is going in the wrong direction, your first appointment with a counselor, your first day in rehab, your decision to let go of an old way of living and embark on a new one. Everything is confusing. Everything is uncertain. We have a deep sense of discontinuity and a loss of confidence. The experience of newness at times can be exciting—a new car, a new house, a new reclining chair, a new television—but for most of us, this change, this transformation, is deeply uncomfortable. For instance, the Covid-19 pandemic has been and was a time of massive transformation, which is what made it so unbearable for so many.

The *struggle of transformation* is perfectly captured in almost every biblical story, but none so clearly as the whole book of Exodus. Moses lives in comfort in Pharaoh's house, but his killing of an Egyptian leads him to flee into the desert, where he undergoes personal and spiritual transformation. Not only does he adopt a whole new way of living, but it's also where he has a personal experience of God that transforms the purpose of his life. Forty years later, he gathers the Israelites and leads them through forty years of being transformed by their desert experience of following God.

Most Christians don't pick up on this, but the desert is always the place of transformation in the Bible. Think of the list of biblical characters who are transformed through desert/wilderness experiences: Adam and Eve, Abraham, Moses, Elijah, all of the prophets, David, Jesus, Paul (we are told in Galatians 1:17 that Paul went to Arabia—a desert—for three years after his conversion), and finally the Israelites. The desert motif is a strong one in the Bible, for it is the place of transformation—the place where we struggle with loneliness, deprivation, poverty, hunger, thirst, failure, doubt, confusion, sorrow, uncertainty, and potentially death. Even the stories of the Bible that don't center on the desert—Noah, Isaac/Israel, Joseph, Samson,

Gideon, all of the disciples who become apostles—are transformed by some sort of desertlike experience, whether it is imprisonment, slavery, constant threat, exile, or occupation.

When we undergo transformation, we experience a period when we don't know what we will become, but we can't go back to where we were. We have no choice but to go forward, and yet, like the Israelites in the desert, we really, really, really want to go back: "And all the Israelites complained against Moses and Aaron; the whole congregation said to them, 'Would that we had died in the land of Egypt! Or would that we had died in this wilderness! Why is the Lord bringing us into this land to fall by the sword? Our wives and our little ones will become booty; would it not be better for us to go back to Egypt?'" (Num 14:2–3).

When people are undergoing transformation, they are fragile. They're anxious. They become resistant, especially if the transformation feels threatening or confusing because of how much of what and who they are is being let go. This was the dilemma faced by the prophets. They came forth from the desert, calling for transformation to a highly resistant people who were worried about losing all they had. Often their messages built up stronger resistance, since the criticism made the Jews defensive. In contrast, the apostles built up relationships, which reduced resistance and in the process helped lead people to their eventual *reformation*.

Something that most therapists, spiritual directors, and life, executive, and clergy coaches understand intuitively is that overcoming resistance is central to the work they do as they lead people through transformation. The reality of resistance is also understood to some degree by teachers, consultants, military officers, business leaders, and parents. They understand that any kind of success comes after an intentional process of transformation where people are made to feel safe and are guided through the transforming process. If we are too aggressive in our attempt to change them, their resistance will turn into some form of defensiveness—repression, projection, denial, rationalization, generalization, avoidance, blaming, or something else. Once this happens, they become like Ahab and Jezebel in the face of the prophet Elijah (1 Kgs 18–19), scheming to get rid of us (or worse). Those who lead others to be transformed understand the nature of resistance. They build trust and connection that overcome resistance. This is a reason therapy often takes so long. It takes time to build up a trust that eventually allows for transformation. I believe the apostles fundamentally understood resistance, especially since they were forming communities of Jews and gentiles, slave and free, male and female.

Eventually, if we are able to navigate the ambivalence and turmoil of transformation, we become *reformed*. We become something just a little bit new, which then becomes our new formation (which will eventually become transformed and reformed in the future).

So should we aim for massive personal and spiritual transformation and reformation in each sermon? We can try, but that puts us back in the mode of trying to be merely prophetic. It's as though we have only one sermon through which to transform them. In reality, we preach almost every Sunday, so each Sunday becomes a time of transformation. We don't have to do it all at once. This is why the relationship is so important—it keeps them coming back with a mindset that's open to being transformed each Sunday.

One of the things that van Kaam emphasizes is that although spiritual transformation is always ongoing, the most successful transformations are often those that he calls "just noticeable improvements," or JNIs.[3] Often we want grand transformations. We want our sermons to dramatically change listeners' lives each Sunday, but the reality is that the larger the transformation attempted, the greater the resistance against it. Again, this was the struggle of the prophets. They

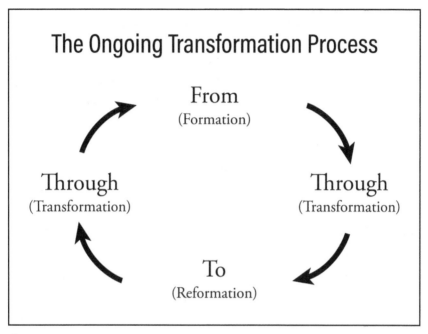

Figure 2.

came out from the desert asking everyone to change everything. The apostles were different. They moved into these ancient communities and, through a slow process of building relationships, led gentiles and Jews, men and women, free and slave through transformation and reformation. This transformation was rarely sudden. People's initial conversion may have been sudden, but their ongoing transformation and reformation was a matter of going from JNI to JNI.

The key takeaway from this discussion is that each sermon we give on a Sunday morning is potentially a JNI-transforming and JNI-reforming event. When we are truly transformational in our preaching, we are intentional about helping people map out a path to reformation. In the process, we have to clearly help them recognize and navigate their resistance in order to become open to being reformed.

Transformational Preaching

The key difference between prophetic and apostolic preaching is that the former aims to create quick, massive change to highly resistant people and the latter aims to slowly, constantly, and sensitively change people over time. The more intentional we are about this kind of sensitive, relational, and ongoing transformation through our weekly messages, the more likely it is that our members will experience a subtle yet significant transformation of life over time. For example, one of our church members said to me, "I don't know that I've heard you preach much about racism, but I realize that since you've been here, I've changed my thinking 180 degrees."

Transforming sermons are structured by using a simple *from-through-to* formula, which corresponds to formation-transformations-reformation. They acknowledge where people are coming *from* and what that life is like where they are. They speak to ways of living and being that they are being called *to* and the possibilities of that life. Finally, they offer guidance for moving *through* the struggles they will face as they undergo transformation.

It's difficult to capture what this means without an example, so let me share with you a short, simple transforming sermon:

> I don't know about you, but I've struggled with impatience all of my life. I've really had to work on it. I was that kid in the marshmallow experiment who would have grabbed the one marshmallow instead of delaying gratification and getting two. I had such a hard time waiting for good things to happen. As a result, when I was in fourth grade, my great impatience led to *death*!
>
> We had been told in school that if we picked up some caterpillars, put them in a jar with small holes drilled into the cap,

and then added a small twig with leaves attached, the caterpillar would build a cocoon and become a butterfly.

That sounded great! I diligently collected a jar, a twig, and a caterpillar and put together my butterfly kit. My caterpillar soon wrapped itself in a cocoon. Then I waited, and waited, and waited. I couldn't stand it. What was taking that stupid caterpillar so long to turn into a butterfly? I felt sorry for it. It was stuck in the cocoon. It had to be dark and gloomy in there. It probably wanted to be done with the darkness. So out of both pity and impatience, I pulled out the twig and slowly cut open the cocoon with an X-Acto knife. I expected a beautiful butterfly to fly out. Instead, there was this black, gooey thing that looked nothing like a caterpillar or a butterfly, and I couldn't put it all back together. I had killed it! I was really sad and disappointed. Even today I feel guilty for killing that butterfly . . . the caterpillar . . . the butterpillar, or whatever it was.

Butterflies are symbols of Christian life, and those reasons become clearer as we think about how caterpillars become butterflies. Have you ever thought about the fundamental difference between a caterpillar and a butterfly? It's not whether or not they fly; it's what they contribute to life.

Caterpillars are basically destructive infants. Once hatched, they eat leaves. An army of caterpillars can actually kill a tree by consuming its leaves. Caterpillars, just by being caterpillars, *harm* life. Butterflies *give* life. They sip the nectar flowers give them, and in response, they give life back by spreading pollen from plant to plant. Caterpillars are life taking. Butterflies are life giving. We are called to become like butterflies, to give life, but the problem is that we are often stuck, or even content, being caterpillars.

You know what I mean. How often have we been destructive because we have focused only on ourselves? We consume and consume and consume, not worrying about how it impacts everyone else. We consume resources, we consume entertainment, we consume people's efforts, and we rarely consider the consequences. In relationships, when the focus is only on us, we end up harming the people around us. In work, when it's all about us, we tear down those around us. In our culture, we care only about what's in it for us. With the earth, we care only about how things impact us and not how what we're doing may be creating more floods, wildfires, and hurricanes; melting ice caps and permafrost; and more.

Christian faith doesn't call us to live merely as caterpillars. It calls us to transformation. It calls us to become life giving, not life taking. That call isn't an easy one to respond to, because it's an invitation to begin a journey that may lead us through darkness and uncertainty. As Christians, we're constantly called to become transformed—to enter dark periods that can change who we are. None of us likes that, though, because these transformations can be painful, *and we hate pain.*

Jesus never taught that we won't suffer. Instead, he taught that our suffering can be transformed into healing, just as his crucifixion and resurrection were transforming and healing. The Christian life isn't about how to avoid pain; it's about how we can transform that pain into blessings. For example, some of us will go through a divorce. The Christian question isn't necessarily, How do we never get divorced? Sometimes divorces do happen and should happen. The Christian question is, How can we use our painful experiences to become more caring and compassionate to others who go through turmoil, and how can we use what we've learned to improve our relationships in the future? If we get fired from a job, can we use that experience to make other people's work experiences better? If we are recovering from an addiction, can we become butterflies in our recovery and use our experiences to make other people's lives better? Can we emerge from times of political and national division to become people who strive to bring about healing and community?

The struggle is that this transformation is painful. We always want to go back to what life was like before all of this. But the life of faith is a life of hope. It teaches us that if we're willing to be patient and trust God, good things will be coming, as long as we're brave enough to walk forward. We just can't be like a fourth-grade Graham.

Life is about transformation. It's about letting go of our destructive caterpillar selves so that we can become life-giving butterflies. If you are in the midst of transformation, here are a few things to keep in mind. First, God may be leading you through this transformation, so focus on what God is leading you to become no matter how painful the process is. Second, the pain you're feeling is difficult, but emerging through that pain may make you better able to relieve the pain of others, so look for how you are being taught to be life giving to others. Finally, don't assume God isn't with you. Assume God is, and stay open to God in faith, hope, and love. Amen.

There were a number of things I did in this short sermon (such as using a story and a metaphor to make a point as well as keeping the idea simple, all of which we'll explore in chapter 6), but here's the basic thing: I constructed it as a *from-through-to* sermon (although the *through* part was actually at the end, not the middle). I used the Christian symbol of the butterfly as my metaphor, but it was about transformation and reformation. I can summarize the sermon very simply as a *from-through-to* sentence: *We often live destructive, life-taking lives, but when we seek God, even in our suffering, God will transform us into life givers.*

The simplicity of the sermon idea helps, as we'll discuss in a future chapter. The key, though, is that I spoke about where our lives may be right now—we may focus on self in a way that consumes life from others. I spoke about what God seeks for us to become—how we will *be reformed*. I spoke about the reality of the *transforming* struggle, offering assurances that it's worth it while also pointing out that the pain and uncertainty we feel as we go *through* it is part of the path.

Too often in preaching, we don't pay attention to the detailed steps of the transformation we are really calling our congregants through. Everything in preaching is about transformation. Are we attracted to social justice preaching? Then we need to pay attention to where people are now—their present formation—and what gets in the way of them embracing a more just way of thinking and living. We need to be clear about the transformation we want them to undergo, offering them opportunities to eventually live in a reformed way. We need to be sensitive to the painful transformation they may have to go through and give them guidance on how to do it. Transformative preaching understands that people are resistant by nature, and it sensitively helps them navigate through the uncertainty of transformation (which heightens resistance) on the way to being reformed.

Preparing to Be Transforming

When I was being trained to preach, much of the training focused on doing the exegetical, theological work necessary to deliver a compelling, erudite sermon. Being a Presbyterian, that meant taking one year each of Greek and Hebrew and any number of classes focused on biblical exegesis and understanding. Presbyterians have among the highest standards for biblical scholarship, which I really value. I've always been proud that we Presbyterians are overrepresented in the field of biblical scholarship. I believe that a grounding in the historical-critical method is truly important for preaching because it allows us to interpret Scripture as though we were really there, observing the situation the biblical writers were addressing. Still, preaching is about transformation and reformation, not exegesis and explication, and we Presbyterians are underrepresented in the field of spiritual transformation.

Digging into the background of a biblical passage is important because it helps us hear God speaking through the passage. But the moment we substitute that intellectual work for spiritual insight about God's calling and will for us today is the moment our preaching ceases to be transforming. It becomes merely *informing*. The challenge of being transformational is not confusing biblical and theological *information* for transformation. Informational preaching looks and sounds a lot like transformational preaching. We explore the history underlying a passage, offer theological insights on the passage, and then offer traditional religious explanations and platitudes that root people in basic Christian lessons. We use the passage to give them *information* about themselves, life, and God without ever really engaging them in a deeper, transforming engagement with themselves, life, and God. In other words, we get them thinking *about* God but never push them to an engagement *with* God.

Much of mainline preaching is informational. We tell people the underlying history of a passage—who wrote it, when it was written, who it was written to, what were the theological issues the passage addresses, and why it was written. We help them reflect theologically on the meaning of the passage. We tell them stories related to the passage. But because what we preach never really moves beyond the level of the head into the heart, it remains merely interesting information that never truly transforms. We come away just knowing more. Too often exegetical preaching becomes merely informational preaching. Before you rise to defend the honor of biblical exegesis, let me explain.

Several years ago, I heard a sermon preached by a biblical scholar on Luke 7:36–50. This is the story of the sinful woman who comes into the Pharisee Simon's house and washes Jesus's feet with her tears and hair. The scholar did a very good job of talking about the passage. He told us that the sinful woman wasn't really Mary Magdalene, as many portray her, but simply a woman in need of forgiveness. He told us about the tradition of Jews at the time whereby they invited special guests to dinner yet kept their households open so that even strangers could walk in and visit their guests. He talked about what conditions might have caused her to be considered a sinner. He talked about how the Pharisees were supposed to have welcomed Jesus with hospitality, but the sinful woman did more than them. In the end, he told us that this was a passage about how we are to care for those on the margins. His sermon was full of biblical *information* but short on *transformation* and *reformation* because it never explored the obstacles to caring for those on the margins and what we need to undergo to become more caring and compassionate.

There was nothing wrong with his interpretation though. To me, it was a typical Presbyterian sermon. Clearly, I heard a lot of information about the passage. He did a great job of giving us biblical background, but it was thin in guiding us through whatever transformation he wanted from us. His conclusion came off more as a platitude than guidance. Less time on the *information* and more time on how to transform and reform our lives to be more hospitable would have made all the difference. How could he have made this sermon transforming?

The answer lies not so much in the execution as it does in the preparation. If the sermon preparation had been more transformational, the sermon might have been too. When I first started my ministry at Calvin Presbyterian Church, I used to follow a discipline in sermon preparation—a discipline seminary had trained me for. Fridays would be my prep day. I would read the passage I had selected. Then I would read through commentaries relating to the passage. I would dig into the words, the background, the history, the context, the situation, the author, the audience, and more. I would spend about two to three hours in study. After lunch I would summarize all the historical and theological lessons I had learned in those commentaries. I would try to craft a sentence capturing all of it (often these would be quite complex sentences) as the outline for my sermon. Then I would start to write my sermon, struggling to figure out how to get everything I had discovered through my research into it. My sermons back then were erudite, complex, perfectly reasoned, and looooooong.

After a few years of this, I had an epiphany: Where was the Spirit in my sermons? Was I repeating what scholars had to say, or was I listening for what Christ had to say specifically to me and through me to others? Eventually, I revamped my method. I stopped reading the commentaries as sermon prep. I *would* read commentaries and books by scholars on my own, but not for sermon prep—only for my own growth. The exception was when exploring the biblical background could be transforming. Also, every once in a while, I would go to a commentary if I didn't understand a passage, but that was always in service of helping me listen for God's voice in the passage, not for what to say in the sermon (although periodically, what a commentary had to say did get into the sermon).

To prepare for my sermons, I started out in prayer earlier in the week. I would read the passage several times and ask what God was saying to me through the passage. I would try to prayerfully hear what I sensed was the essential, *transformational* message for me and for others. How was God transforming me through this passage? What lesson was God teaching me about my life and life in general? I would write down what I heard. Then I would ask in prayer, "How are you calling me to preach this to the congregation? What would help them hear what I've heard?" My focus would then be on how to craft this message—this transformational message—for the congregation.

The point is that I was not only crafting a transformational message but also engaging in a transformational process that began with being open to being transformed and reflecting on my own transformational experiences. I spent time delving into the message I had heard through Scripture and asked questions: What's the transformation we're being called into? What holds everyone else and me back from undergoing it? What makes it difficult, and what would nurture it? What stories or metaphors or symbols or pictures or movie clips or experiences or biblical, exegetical explanations would help in talking about this transformation?

If you go back to the short, transformational sermon I shared above, it is a smaller version of an Easter sermon I did in 2004. What I left out was the part about how the resurrection shows us that God is always transforming life takers into life givers, despair into joy, impossibility into possibility, and devastation into restoration. Prior to that original Easter sermon, I spent the earlier parts of the week prayerfully asking, God, what are you calling me to preach? As I did, the image of the butterfly kept coming into my mind. I kept dismissing it as too trite but then decided to reflect on it more, and that's when I got the image of gypsy moth caterpillars denuding trees, which then turned into how even butterfly caterpillars denude trees. From there it was just a question of how to put this transformational message using the metaphor together for Easter Sunday.

So how might I have redone the scholar's sermon about the sinful woman I mentioned above? I probably would have focused less on the background of the passage and more on how God is using it to transform and reform us. I might have contrasted Simon's hubris with the woman's humility and how she used her time with Jesus to become healed, while Simon used his time with Jesus to gain admiration and status for having Jesus the rock star to dinner. I might explore how ignorance and arrogance kill us spiritually, turning life into a pursuit of image making—what we might call Kardashian Christianity—while humility nurtures us spiritually by turning life into a pursuit of compassionate service to Christ in everything we do. I might talk about what feeds arrogance and what feeds humility. I might teach people how they can strive for a humbler life. If I wanted to preach a more social justice–focused sermon, I might emphasize how Jesus was willing to stop what he was doing to really, deeply care about this woman on the margins and his challenge to his hosts to be more caring. I also might discuss what gets in the way of us caring about people like her and what we can do in life to become more compassionate like Jesus rather than indifferent like the Pharisee.

A key concept I learned as a spiritual director comes into play here. I was taught that the good spiritual director always is focusing on obstacles and facilitating conditions. In other words, what obstacles inhibit transformation, and what conditions facilitate it? This is a key part of preaching transformative and reformative sermons. We pay attention to what obstacles to growth trap people where they are. We point them out clearly but gently so that they can become aware of them. These obstacles can be emotional (fear, anxiety, a need to prove ourselves, overriding ambition, and more); historical (our upbringing, our baggage, our cultural history, or familial and social norms and taboos); or practical (lack of resources, lack of power, or lack of access). Then we explore what would help people undergo transformation. What would facilitate it? We focus on what steps they can take, no matter how small or insignificant they may be.

Part of how I changed my sermon preparation came from listening to an interview with a popular Pentecostal pastor whose actual sermon I was kind of meh about. The interviewer asked him, "How many hours a week do you work on a sermon?" "Probably fifteen, twenty," he replied. "Does that include writing it out in your manuscript?" "Oh no, I would never write out my sermon!" "No? Why not?" the interviewer asked incredulously. "Well, if I write out my sermon, then there's no room for the Spirit to speak through me. All the work I do during the week is so that on Sunday, I can be an open window for the Spirit to blow through." I'm always skeptical of pastors who talk about creating room for the Spirit, but I think his point is still valid. We can overprepare for a sermon in ways that inhibit our openness to the Spirit, whether in our preparation, writing, or delivery. Still, I began to look for ways to be less academic in my approach and more open spiritually to what I might be guided to say and teach. I cared less about informing them and more about transforming them. This can mean simplifying sermons and making them less academic and more personal.

Often, master-level pastors feel that if they don't do all the scholarly work for a sermon and subsequently preach an academic-sounding sermon, they're doing something wrong. Academic foundations for sermons aren't bad, but they become problematic when we substitute pedantic, descriptive, abstract academic reasoning for an openness to God's transforming voice within the passage. When our sermons become theological exhortations, academic explorations, and abstract explanations, they cease to be transforming for others. People tune out because they can't connect the sermons with their deepest questions, struggles, and yearnings.

Transformation, Meaning, and Purpose

As we conclude, we have a question to answer: What does transformation have to do with those walking away from the church? The answer comes in noticing what people walking away from church are walking toward. They're reading, listening, and watching transformative books, podcasts, and videos. What they're reading, listening to, and watching feels deeply meaningful and purposeful for them. They just decreasingly find what we offer to be meaningful and purposeful. People live their lives in pursuit of meaning and purpose, and they will gravitate toward those whose ideas seem to lead them there. Or if they can't find those whose ideas lead them there, they'll wallow in shallowness and seek entertainment. Ultimately, transformational preaching offers people guidance that leads them to a greater sense of meaning and purpose—to feel as though the pastor "is preaching about me." When a worshipper thinks that, it becomes self-motivating, and she or he wants to come back again to worship because she or he feels transformed.

The organizational researcher and writer Daniel H. Pink has explored how feeling a sense of meaning and purpose in any idea, activity, or experience becomes intrinsically rewarding and thus leads the person to want more. He says that we have entered an age of "motivation 3.0," an age when people are seeking a rewarding life that satisfies "our innate need to direct our own lives, to learn and create new things, and to do better by ourselves and our world."[4] He contrasts this kind of motivation to what he calls motivations 1.0 and 2.0. Motivation 1.0 is punishment—if you don't do what I want, I will hurt you. Motivation 2.0 is carrot and stick—if you don't do what I want, I will hurt you, but if you do what I want, I will reward you. Christians who criticize with hellfire and damnation while enticing with heavenly paradise are engaging in motivation 2.0. Its ultimate focus is compliance: comply with my theological viewpoint and stay part of my church, and you will avoid punishment and be rewarded.

We have left the age when Christianity could rely on motivational preaching 2.0 and entered an era when people are seeking preaching that subscribes to motivation 3.0. Preaching 2.0 doesn't work with the younger generations because they aren't afraid of going to hell if they don't come to church, and they don't believe they'll gain entry to paradise by coming to church. They are motivated by elements beyond self-preservation. They are motivated by deeper elements that Pink says make any activity intrinsically motivating: autonomy, mastery, and purpose.[5]

The first of these self-motivators is *autonomy.* This is the "innate capacity for self-direction," which is inherently self-rewarding and therefore powerfully motivating.[6] We feel accountable not to others but to something that is self-transcending. We feel a sense of personal independence and responsibility that motivates us. Sermons that teach people how to live self-transcendently and give them guidance on how to achieve it entice people to come back for more because they feel more equipped to live a more positive, purposeful life.

Mastery is the ability to develop satisfying skills that over time give us a sense of confidence. Anyone who has gone to graduate school understands this. It's why we call that first level in a field of study a "master's" degree. We "master" a field that helps us succeed. Sermons that nurture mastery teach people how to develop skills that they then can use to transform themselves, others, and the world. Perhaps we preach in a way that teaches people how to hear God's call to engage in ministry and mission and to develop the courage to follow. Perhaps we teach them basic skills on how to adopt a more prayerful life. Perhaps we teach them how to pragmatically care for others. Perhaps we teach them how to overcome conflict with others and how to soothe conflicts within themselves. Whatever the skills we teach are, they are transforming and reforming because as we exercise mastery, we change. The skills we teach don't need to be sophisticated to be profoundly transforming. For example, teaching people how to simply use breathing in prayer is a sermon teaching mastery.

Great sermons give people a sense of *autonomy* in that they make them aware of God's unique call to them. They give people a sense of *mastery* by teaching them how to concretely do what God's calling them to do—how to pray, how to hear God, how to respond to God, how to be sensitive to people's needs, how to respond to their need, how to live compassionately, and much more. Ultimately, though, great sermons give people a sense of *purpose* by helping them transform into a better version of themselves, and this transformation allows them to live more meaningful lives.

"The most deeply motivated people—not to mention those who are most productive and satisfied—hitch their desires to a cause larger than themselves."[7] Sermons that are intrinsically motivating captivate people in a way that makes listening and reflecting their own reward because they lead people to embrace causes greater than themselves.

Transformative preaching points people to ways of living, ways of responding to the world, ways of discovering God's presence, ways of changing themselves that ultimately lead them to feel as though they are making a difference in the world. When people are given guidance on how to transcend themselves and seek a greater purpose in life, that becomes self-motivating.

I believe that many walking away from the church are seeking this kind of self-transcendence, and the church isn't helping them discover it. We offer creeds, we offer platitudes, we offer doctrine, we offer scriptural interpretations, but we're not always offering paths to self-transcendence. You may argue that we do and that people are lazy. I'll simply counter that if we did, people wouldn't be walking away and looking for those paths elsewhere. In a culture of people who see themselves as spiritual but not religious, they experience what we offer not as transcendent and transforming but as merely religious.

Exercise for Creating a Transformative Sermon

The following is an exercise to create a foundational template for a sermon that engages people to move *from* their current state of being and thinking, *through* the challenges faced in undergoing transformation, and *to* a reformation of their lives (even if it's a JNI):

1. Select the passage for the sermon, either using the lectionary or choosing one that supports a homiletical topic. For example, perhaps focus on Philippians 3:4–14 (the lectionary passage for the week I initially wrote this chapter).
2. Read the passage spiritually and reflectively rather than merely theologically and academically.
   a. Read it slowly and prayerfully.
   b. Ask the question throughout, "God, what are you saying to me about my life and my church through this passage?"

   For example, I heard the idea that Paul offers guidance for our polarized times through his guidance to the Philippians about how to overcome the Jew/gentile polarization in new churches.
   c. Write down whatever thoughts, insights, and inspirations come to you.
   d. Put your notes aside and continue to reflect on the passage for a few days, jotting down insights and inspirations.

   If you feel the need to get more information on the passage, consult commentaries and other resources. But make

sure that you do so in the service of hearing what God is saying to you through them rather than focusing on ways you can use their insights for your sermon. Make this background information part of your prayerful reflection. (For example, I used a commentary to learn more about the Jewish/gentile split in the Philippian church.)

3. Reflect on your passage in a *from-through-to* way, and jot down insights gained from your reflections:

   a. Reflect on the *reformation* you believe the passage is inviting you and others to embrace.

      For example, I focused on putting aside our own beliefs and biases to see life from the perspective of those Christians who disagree with us.

   b. Reflect on the state most people and you are in that creates resistance to transformation—their current *formation*.

      For example, I thought about our tendency to value only our own customs, perspectives, and beliefs because we're ignorant about those of others.

   c. Identify the obstacles and conditions that obstruct or aid people in going through *transformation*. Be clear about the emotions surrounding the ambivalence people might feel if they are to undergo transformation.

      For example, obstacles I identified included hubris about being "right," certainty that God is on our side, and fearing and devaluing those who are different, while facilitating conditions I named were looking at issues from others' perspectives and honoring others' experiences, perspectives, and beliefs in the way we hope they will ours.

4. When you are ready to craft the sermon, take your notes and write a *from-through-to* sentence. (These elements can be reordered.) Identify and articulate succinctly the following:

    a. The state most people are in is _____.

    b. The transformative struggle is _____.

    c. The reformation you are calling them to adopt is _____

    _____.

    Here's a sample sentence: We are polarized because we fear others who are not like us, but if we are willing to deeply understand their experiences and perspectives, we will eventually love and treat them as Christ loves and treats us.

5. Use that *from-through-to* sentence as the outline of your sermon. The order of your sermon can vary but should clearly capture in discourse, story, symbol, metaphor, or another way the three elements:

    a. The state people are in that Christ is calling them to move away from

    b. The struggles and challenges of transformation that Christ is calling them to undergo

    c. The reformation Christ is calling them to adopt

6. Refine your sermon by continuing to hone those elements you think are essential to helping listeners transform.

CHAPTER 3

PREACHING IN A POSTMODERN AGE

I made an agreement with my father as a condition to being part of my confirmation class. I could walk away from the church, but to do so, I had to stand before the church session (the Presbyterian term for the board) and tell them I was choosing to leave. My father's message? No slinking away. You stand for your decisions. So I left the church at age fifteen, vowing never to return. Reflecting on the reasons I left the church at age fifteen and returned at age twenty-four, my mind always goes to one particular prayer and one particular sermon.

I'll start with the prayer from my childhood that provided a path for my eventual return. It touched me deeply and kept me slightly open to church, even when I was most church averse. I was about ten or eleven years old. Sitting in the balcony of the Episcopal church I attended periodically with my mother and stepfather, I was trans-fixed by the candles, the stained glass, and an ineffable sense of the holy, even as I ignored the sermon, hymns, and other "talky" stuff. Eventually, it came time for communion. I walked up to the rail with my mother. Being too young to receive communion, I knelt beside her with my arms resting on the communion rail. She received the elements from the rector. He then looked at me, asked my name, and placed his hand on my head while saying a prayer of blessing over me. Something happened to me in that moment. I was blessed! I had no idea what that meant, but it mattered. I was blessed! I walked away marveling at it and reflected on it the rest of the day. Apparently, I'm still reflecting on it.

That experience stood in complete contrast to another experience I had several years later in the Presbyterian church I attended after moving across the state to live with my father and stepmother (an experience I mentioned in more detail earlier). I was a few years older but just as distracted. Again, I was paying more attention to the stained glass, candles, and crosses, but now I at least tried to listen to the sermon because, well, that's what we were supposed to do.

It came time for the sermon. The pastor slowly walked up to the pulpit. Pausing after his stodgy prayer, he gazed at us over his half-moon glasses (I found out much later that he was only in his midthirties at the time, but I thought he was seventy by the way he walked and talked) and proceeded to preach a traditional Reformed sermon. He spoke forcefully about how totally depraved we are, how we have done nothing to deserve God's love, and how only by God's grace do we have a sliver of a chance in the afterlife. As a seventh grader, that sermon cemented my opinion—I want nothing to do with church in the future if that's how he thinks God is. What he was preaching ran counter to a number of experiences of God in my childhood. I wasn't going to let this pastor and church influence me. There was no blessing in him. I now felt cursed and rejected.

So what was the essential difference between the two events? You'll probably think, "One was positive, the other negative." That would be true, but there's more depth to it. The first experience was a *postmodern* religious experience that touched me, a postmodern kid. The second was a *modernist* one spiced with *premodern* overtones that clanged off my ears. If this paragraph leaves you a little bit mystified regarding what's postmodern, modern, and premodern, please bear with me, because I believe understanding the difference and adapting to our now postmodern world is the only way Christian preaching will reach those walking away. It's for this reason that I believe this chapter may be the most important one in this book.

Preaching effectively and compellingly to the ever-expanding cadre of nones and dones and to the expanding ranks of the spiritual but not religious is a growing challenge for the mainline church. Unfortunately, we're not doing it particularly well, as our numbers continue to decline. Meanwhile, all sorts of movements outside Christianity and the traditional religions are reaching them effectively and compellingly. Most aren't religious in nature, but they provide adherents with a sense of purpose, meaning, direction, community, and more. Nones, dones, and the spiritual but not religious baffle us. We've tried our best to reach them by improving the quality of our worship, ministry, mission, and preaching, but it's failing. Our dilemma reminds me of something said to me years ago by a pastor of a struggling church: "We're trying to find a really good organist. We've realized that one reason we're losing younger people is that the woman playing our organ isn't good enough. We need someone more inspiring. Do you know of anyone who can make full use of our wonderful organ?"

I responded simply, "Umm, not that I know of." I didn't share what was in my head: "Seriously? You want a better organist to reach those folks? It doesn't matter how good your organist is. Every day they listen to music in their homes, their cars, and stores, music played with keyboards, guitars, drums, bass, and more, and you're trying to attract them with your organ?!" Mainline preaching is similar, in many ways, to striving for excellent organ playing. We've learned a style of preaching designed for a previous era, and it's become partly responsible for our congregants walking away. If you love traditional preaching, then what I've said feels harsh in the same way church-loving people react when I tell them I detest the organ.

We've Entered a New Age

So what was so fundamentally, era-relatedly different between my blessing experience and my cranky-preacher experience? One led to an experience of God. The other shut it off. The blessing helped me feel God's presence. The sermon basically said, "There's no experience coming because God has very little interest in you, and you're going to experience God only if God has a wee bit of time to spare you a crumb of grace." You personally may not preach the way the pastor from my youth did, but that's not really the issue. The issue is whether your preaching leads to an experience of God or not. That's the difference between a modern and postmodern sermon.

Over years of trying to understand what postmodernism is, I've been confronted with a barrage of confusing definitions from writers who seem better at saying what postmodernism isn't rather than what it is. The writer who really helped me understand postmodernism and how to approach it from a religious perspective was Ken Wilber. Wilber is a fascinating man and prolific writer. He is a college dropout—first from Duke University and then from the University of Nebraska. He dropped out in order to engage in a more intensive study of *everything*. He embarked on a decades-long study of philosophy, religion, theology, psychology, sociology, and more. In the process, he has sought to create an integrative understanding of life. As a result, he's become one of the great postmodern writers of the past twenty years.

The book of his that helped me understand the postmodern versus modern and premodern eras is *Marriage of Sense and Soul*.[1] In it, he attempts to understand how science and religion can and should be integrated. Unlike many authors who choose one field over the other (which is a very modernist thing to do) or who merely see them as dealing with different realms of reality (also modernist), Wilber sees science and religion as intrinsically, integrally related with each other. He believes that postmodern thinking is the only way to integrate the two. I won't be exploring the relationship between science and religion in this chapter, but I will cull insights from his thinking to explore how to preach to those walking away—to those *postmodern* people who struggle to resonate with our sermons. To help you understand Wilber's insights, I first need to get you thinking about two of the biggest initial purveyors of postmodernism—Picasso and Einstein.

Have you ever looked at a Picasso painting and wondered, "What the _____ is going on here?" His art seems to make no sense. For example, I invite you to google his 1931 painting *Marie-Thérèse, face et profil*. Picasso was a classically trained artist who could easily have made his career creating "normal" paintings. Why paint this one? It's ugly. It's disjointed. It's confusing. It is also fundamentally postmodern. What makes it postmodern?

If you look at it front on, as we typically do, it looks like a disjointed portrait. Viewing any painting from a "front-on" perspective is a typically *modernist* way of viewing it, which is why this painting is so confusing. If you want to understand the postmodern perspective, cover the left side of her face. She's now facing to the left. Cover the right. She's now facing right, but her eye remains on us. Take the hand away. She's facing front. Picasso painted three different perspectives in one portrait, unlike the *Mona Lisa*, which requires us to look from merely one perspective—the front. Leonardo da Vinci's masterpiece was tremendous because it showed depth—the soft landscape over one shoulder versus the hazy one over the other shoulder makes it a three-dimensional painting—but it's still modernist. Picasso painted people from many perspectives. He was obsessed with all sorts of perspectives, and not just reality-based ones. He revealed a deeper truth by expanding our perspectives and encouraging us to realize that life is made up of a myriad of perspectives, all valid and all revealing some level of reality and truth.

Einstein did something similar, but not through art. In many ways, Einstein was the primary theorist for quantum theory, although he hated it. He considered himself to be Newtonian (someone who believed in fixed "laws" of nature and reality), yet he provided the theories that opened the way to alternative, quantum perspectives. He did this first through his special theory of relativity and then by his general theory of relativity ($E = MC^2$). Both theories demonstrated that what we see as reality is relative to the situation and context. These theories ushered in an age of quantum awareness.

His theories of relativity can be captured in the simple thought experiment he did while serving as a Swiss patent office worker. As he stared out the window at the train station next door and watched trains enter and exit, he imagined what it was like to be on those trains. He imagined himself tossing a ball up in the air and catching it while riding in the train as it rushed through the Swiss countryside. Then he imagined opening the window, putting his arm out, and tossing the ball up. It would fly backward. With a sudden "Eureka!" he realized that the reality of physics within the train was different from that outside the train and that time and space within the train were different from that outside of it. Reality was relative to the context. This led him to grasp that the passage of time for those traveling at the speed of light is slower than for those traveling at lower speeds. Thus, he theorized that time is *relative*, depending on gravity and velocity (those are the *M* and *C* of his formula). We think of time as an immutable constant, yet it is dependent on our context—the speed at which we're moving and the gravity exerted on us. So, for example, time will be different on our spinning planet, rotating around the sun, which is rotating around the core of our galaxy, than it is in a fixed position between galaxies. This led many to realize that truth is perspectival, not fixed.

Like Picasso, Einstein demonstrated that our perspectives matter. Hence time on earth is different from time on Pluto or on a planet in a different part of our galaxy. The earth is spinning on its axis at a certain speed and traveling around the sun at a certain distance and speed, as our solar system spins around the core of the galaxy at a certain speed from the outside, and as the galaxy moves through space.

So what do Picasso and Einstein have to do with preaching in a postmodern way? The postmodern era is one that acknowledges, values, and embraces a variety of perspectives on and experiences of truth. In essence, postmodern people recognize that while there may be an ultimate truth, we can't ascertain it from merely one perspective. We need to integrate different perspectives if we are to truly discover deeper truths.

It's a mistake to describe the postmodern era as one of cynical deconstruction. Those who simply deconstruct beliefs about reality and truth aren't truly postmodern. They're just disgruntled modernists who have taken either a nihilist or a critical view of everything except their closely cherished personal truth. At its extreme, deconstruction is an endless abyss that leads to nothing because it simply tears down truth. It never offers truth. My younger brother, Jim, perfectly embodied this in his late teenage years whenever we discussed any idea he disagreed with. He'd say, "How do you know? You're not God!"

Wilber says that the idea that because everything is relative, everything then must be deconstructed has "been blown radically out of proportion by the extremist wing of postmodernism, and the result is a totally deconstructed world that takes deconstructionists with them."[2] In other words, to be postmodern isn't to be cynical and skeptical and nihilistic. It means to be willing to look at truth from different—perhaps even competing—perspectives, much as Picasso and Einstein did.

For Wilber, the true postmodernist recognizes flaws in certain "fixed" perspectives—especially from those who proclaim to offer "the truth"—while also recognizing that some perceptions on truth are more valid than others, such as those that rely on empirical evidence or those that lead to a better-lived life because they provide a sense of meaning and a more universal moral foundation.

How does this apply to those walking away? Increasingly these are people willing to consider everything from a variety of perspectives in order to embrace a greater truth. They want to integrate insights from science, art, other religions, psychology, philosophy, and more. They may not do it through intentional study. They often do it through social media—Facebook, TikTok, Twitter, YouTube—and through websites, movies, television, music, novels, and more. They are willing to explore a variety of ideas and belief systems and are skeptical and cynical toward those who promote only *one* way of viewing life. This view of truth led a seventh-grade Graham Standish, listening to a one-ultimate-truth sermon on how depraved he is and on how God might offer grace only if *He's* not too busy, to eagerly await the moment he no longer had to go to church. Mind you, that seventh grader was still discovering God's presence through his own past and present experiences. I would later discover that same sense of presence through my exploration of other traditions and religions, all of which eventually led back to the church. The difference was that when I came back to the church, I was willing to integrate a variety of perspectives that *included* the Presbyterian, Reformed one. What made me somewhat of an outlier was that I was willing to do this only on the condition that I would not exclude all others.

The Postmodern, Modern, and Premodern Perspectives

So what are postmodernism, modernism, and premodernism? I want to offer the central premises of each so that when preaching, you can be intentional in how you construct your sermon to reach those walking away. The simplest way of describing the three is this:

- *Premodern.* There is *one* truth, and it resides in the doctrines of the church. All art, morals, and truth must be aligned with the church's doctrines. If they don't, they are heretical.
- *Modern.* There is one truth, but it resides in "our" discipline, tradition, sect, field of study, or body of knowledge, not in theirs. So we must fight over who holds the truth.
- *Postmodern.* There *may* be one truth, but we can't ascertain it from merely one perspective. So we must explore a diversity of perspectives to gain a 360-degree understanding of it in order to discover the deeper truth.

The premodern period existed roughly from the establishment of Christianity as the religion of the Roman Empire in 388 CE until the Renaissance and subsequent Age of Enlightenment, roughly beginning in the twelfth century. The Renaissance, the advent of the modern period, clashed with the premodern by exploring new ideas and pulling away from the church's dominance. Prior to this, all art was religious art. All science and mathematics were used to prove firmly held church doctrine. In this age prior to Copernicus and Galileo, all new discoveries and theories had to be submissive to church doctrine. Hence, the earth could not revolve around the sun because that would violate the church's biblical doctrine of an earth of vaults and pillars and sparkly, heavenly objects placed there by God. Laity could not read Scripture for themselves because it may lead them away from church doctrine. It was reserved only for those trained in doctrine. Any other competing perspectives must be stamped out, which gave rise to inquisitions, pogroms, and sometimes torture and mass executions.

Premodern preaching offered *one* truth, the church's truth. While the contemporary Roman Catholic Church no longer embraces premodern thinking, it still struggles with the vestiges of it as it grapples with what is and isn't infallible truth. Where we see premodern preaching still alive is in fundamentalist, creationist preaching that offers only one, biblical truth, to which even objective science must be submissive.

Most of today's mainline church preachers have been trained in modernist preaching as they argue with other disciplines, religions, and sects for "truth." In other words, we try to rhetorically prove that our perspective is the true one. The modern era began as art, science, and religion split from church dominance. As Wilber states, "Where previously these spheres tended to be fused, modernity differentiated them and let each proceed at its own pace, with its own dignity, using its own tools, following its own discoveries, unencumbered from the other spheres."[3]

Thus, the great artists such as Michelangelo and da Vinci became freer to explore a more realistic art that veered from highly imaginative, idealized religious art. They would paint portraits and carve sculptures that explored mundane life rather than transcendent, biblical themes. Perhaps that's what makes the *Mona Lisa* so great: we have only the vaguest idea of who she was, what her status in life was, or what she was thinking. She was nobody great, and nobody at that time did paintings of nobodies, thinking about nothing, representing nada. She's a mundane departure from church-inspired art.

This modernist splitting became more prominent as the ensuing centuries passed, with those studying astronomy, biology, medicine, and other disciplines making great discoveries that veered from church doctrine. We see the vestiges of competitive, modernist thinking on college campuses even today among different disciplines, each asserting that they have the true perspective on truth (i.e., hard sciences versus social sciences versus philosophy, although I'm not sure where that leaves computer science and marketing majors).

In the religious realm, the modern age gave rise to a battle for competing truths. During the Reformation, multiple sects popped up, at first in a battle for truth against the Catholic Church. As they matured, they then engaged in a battle for truth against each other. For example, those adhering to the Reformed tradition might have respect for Lutherans' and Mennonites' theologies, but they firmly believed their own theology and subsequent practices were superior and closest to what God really sought. Meanwhile, Lutherans and Mennonites refused to yield ground to the Reformed as they asserted their superiority. Eventually, this competitive battle for truth gave rise to the Anglicans, Presbyterians, Puritans, Quakers, Methodists, Shakers, Huguenots, Amish, Fundamentalists, Pentecostalists, and on and on and on. Each presented themselves, their theology, their practices, and their rituals as superior and closest to God's truth than the others.

This battle for truth sparked the advance of modernist culture, which hit its peak during the twentieth century. Where would we be economically, technically, and even politically without competitive modernity and its entrepreneurial pursuits? The separation of disciplines has allowed for amazing scientific discoveries, technological advances, and even democratic progress because we aren't beholden to "one truth" (such as one religious truth, scientific truth, or artistic truth) that squelches all others.

So what does "modernist" preaching look like? Well, it's what most of us have been trained in. We are taught the doctrines of our traditions, and we're taught to preach in ways that assert and promote our creeds, theologies, and practices. For example, as a Presbyterian, I have been trained to promote and protect Reformed principles such as the "Great Ends of the Church":

the proclamation of the gospel for the salvation of humankind;
the shelter, nurture, and spiritual fellowship of the children of God;
the maintenance of divine worship;
the preservation of the truth;
the promotion of social righteousness; and
the exhibition of the Kingdom of Heaven to the world.[4]

To be Reformed, I'm expected by my Presbyterian tradition to be steeped in this tradition, which I am. In my preaching, I'm supposed to promote and defend a Reformed worldview. I'm responsible for teaching people the Reformed concepts of sinfulness, fallenness, total depravity (remember the sermon I heard in seventh grade?), the sovereignty of God, the primacy of Christ, *sola scriptura*, and more. Those immersed in modernity are immersed in their conclave of truth and demand obedience to it.

Modernist preaching teaches truth and promotes a view that opens people to Christ's salvation as understood by the preacher's tradition. At its best, it provides people with an avenue to discover Christ in their lives as they adopt a particular theological understanding of life and reality. At its worst, it becomes merely what a pastor once said when being examined (to serve a church in a different presbytery from her or his previous one, pastors are required to be questioned and tested by that church's presbytery) by our presbytery to become the pastor of one of our churches. He was asked what he loved best about ministry. He replied, "I love teaching people what they *need to know* to be saved." No one challenged him, despite the Presbyterian emphasis on justification by grace through faith: "Since all have sinned and fall short of the glory of God; they are now justified by his grace as a gift, through the redemption that is in Christ Jesus, whom God put forward as a sacrifice of atonement by his blood, effective through faith" (Rom 3:23–25). In other words, he was certain that salvation was really a matter of holding a certain truth, one he believed he held and was responsible for teaching to others.

So what does postmodern faith look like? To me, it's summed up in something my professor and mentor, Adrian van Kaam, said in a class during my second year of PhD studies: "To be a deeply spiritual person, we have to do two separate, opposite things at the same time. First, we must dig deeply into our own tradition. Second, we must be in constant dialogue with all others." I am unabashedly postmodern. In my own training and background, I have studied psychology, the spirituality of Christianity and other faiths, social work, Protestant and Catholic and Eastern Orthodox theologies, biblical and world history, biology, anthropology, sociology, organizational theory, Buddhism, Taoism, and so much more, yet I am still deeply Presbyterian.

Digging into the insights and practices of our own tradition gives us theological and spiritual depth as the teachings and practices form us. Dialoguing with other traditions reveals the limitations and biases of our own ones. Digging deeply into only our own tradition without the external dialogue traps us by preventing us from distinguishing between what's life giving and what's life sapping about our tradition. Meanwhile, getting to know the perspectives of other traditions without exploring in depth any particular one makes us like spiritual water spiders, never plunging below the surface of a faith tradition to discover the life-giving teachings and practices of that tradition.

This spiritual need for both depth and breadth—for engaging both with a tradition and in dialogue with others—is crucial to understanding how to preach to postmodern people who have walked away from church. They are in touch with, and influenced by, a vast array of divergent belief systems, fields of study, generational values, and philosophical perspectives. Rarely do they hold only one perspective to be true, and they often hold conflicting points of view in tension. For instance, they might be very conservative politically while being extremely liberal in personal sexual behavior. They might have liberal views on gun control while having very libertarian views on marijuana possession. They may believe completely in both evidence-based science toward medicine and anecdote-based, crazy ideas about optimum health. To be postmodern is to hold a variety of perspectives and beliefs that modernist parents and grandparents find baffling. Instead of seeing the world from a modernist, "either this *or* that" point of view toward any argument, they're able to embrace a postmodern, "both this *and* that" perspective. When preaching to these people, we can't just make modernist arguments that proclaim one view to be "the truth." That guarantees we'll be tuned out right off the bat. Preaching to postmoderns requires the ability to reduce their resistance to our ideas by integrating different perspectives in our sermons. In other words, we must look at an issue from a variety of perceptual viewpoints, just as Picasso did. We might express an idea logically and rationally but also use story, film clips, art, poetry, and more. We also might dialogue with other traditions, not to denigrate them, but to show how, for instance, Christian contemplation is related to Buddhist meditation.

If we really want to reach these people, we need to grapple with a variety of perspectives ourselves. We have to study and learn about a whole variety of topics that modernist Christians often have strong opinions about but never really examine. We will need to learn about other denominations and religions from an experiential perspective and not just a theological one. For example, how do their worship and practices nurture faith, life, and the experience of God? We can't just dismiss them. We have to experience them. Are we willing to learn more about Islam, Buddhism, Taoism, the New Age movement, near-death experiences, and more? I mean not just by reading a book but by visiting temples and mosques and other gatherings while engaging in respectful and compassionate discussions with those of other beliefs and practices to discover how their experiences have shaped their lives. Are we willing to learn about science, psychology, anthropology, business organizational theory, and more? Are we willing to learn about other cultures, ethnicities, and races? Are we willing to make friends with those who don't think or believe like us while treating them with respect rather than as potential converts?

Preaching in a postmodern way also requires that we embrace the reality that an era has passed. We've moved from a modernist era to a postmodern one. Many people are actively rejecting churches that they believe are immersed in a competitive, modernist view. We can grieve and lament the passing of one era to the other, from comfort to uncertainty, but if we refuse to adapt, then we need to accept that even more will walk away, leaving us with our dying churches.

Preaching to a Postmodern Generation

The starting point for preaching to a postmodern generation is appreciating and accepting postmodernists' skepticism of absolute-truth claims. If we are going to assert something as absolutely true, they will respond like my brother did: "How do you know? Are you

God? What about this? What about that?" If they are confronted
with a variety of absolute-truth claims, they are more likely to gravitate toward those coming from science than from any other source.
There are two reasons for this: (1) they've been taught that objective,
empirical science is truth, and (2) they've witnessed the breakdown
of religious institutions that proclaimed truth but operated in greedy,
selfish, bigoted, and hypocritical ways. They've witnessed evangelical
pyramid schemes, Roman Catholic pedophilia, and mainline church
irrelevance.

So what are the first steps in constructing a postmodern sermon
that will invite postmodern thinkers back to the church? It comes
through

- exploring contexts,
- embracing a diversity of perspectives,
- helping people prioritize perspectives, and
- emphasizing experience.

Let's start with *exploring contexts*, since that's closest to what most
pastors have been trained in. Pastors who have been trained in the
historical-critical method of biblical scholarship understand how to
explore biblical contexts. Their training in understanding the cultural
and economic situations of the time period in which a passage was
written, who wrote it, what questions or issues it addresses, who the
audience was, and what the societal challenges of the times were is
invaluable to understanding Scripture and making it clearer and more
relevant to today. In fact, we pastors have been trained to understand
the diversity of cultural contexts. The question is whether we can
take that same level of understanding and apply it to *exploring the
contexts* of the culture we're speaking to. Can we understand it not
only from our own theological and spiritual perspectives but also from

psychological, sociological, biological, political, and cultural perspectives? Can we also integrate these into our sermons?

For example, let's pretend we are going to address the thorny issue of whether couples should move in together prior to marriage. You will not get them to stop doing so by simply proclaiming it to be wrong. I discovered the force of this years ago when a couple who lived in another state asked me to perform their wedding. The bride had grown up in our church, and the groom had grown up agnostic but was warming to the idea of going to church because of his exposure to our church. I said yes, but they had to get premarital counseling from a pastor near where they lived together. Part of this was me guiding them to find a church near them that they could become part of.

They began to meet with a pastor near them in a church they were considering joining together. In the first meeting, he chastised them for living together, insisted that she move out, and said that he would find a member of the church she could move in with until their wedding six months from then—all this in the first fifteen minutes. They considered it but eventually rejected the idea as both impractical and unnecessary. They were firmly part of a generation that believed in living together as a precursor to marriage. At the next scheduled meeting, the pastor made them wait half an hour before he showed up. He then hemmed and hawed for fifteen minutes and finally told them that they were living in sin and that he could not help them with their counseling. He then proceeded to proclaim that I was a piss-poor pastor who should immediately give up my ordination. Perhaps you agree, but here was the result of it: The groom decided that all Christians were judgmental hypocrites (but that I was the rare exception to the rule) and that he would never be seduced by Christianity again. She decided that she would stop looking for a church in her community and would simply consider herself a lifelong member of our church, even if she attended only when visiting her family.

I realize that the pastor wasn't "preaching" to them from a pulpit; he was preaching a message to them in his office. What could he have done differently? He could have talked not only about his theology but also about what the field of counseling reveals—that the rate of divorce is significantly higher among those who live together than those who don't prior to marriage. He might have shown a bit of grace to them in understanding the financial reasons they had decided to move in together, which was the primary driver of the decision, aided by their generation's acceptance of premarital cohabitation. He might have focused his counseling on how the lack of commitment by those moving in together erodes future commitment. In the end, they probably wouldn't have agreed, but he might have opened them to what he considered a better perspective of life. He also may have been able to help them solidify their marriage through membership in a marriage- and family-oriented church. Instead, he didn't engage them within their context, and they responded by doing what postmoderns do—they walked away.

This leads us to the second point, which is that as we *embrace a diversity of perspectives*, we invite people to embrace us. Diversity isn't about just race and gender. Diversity is a more global concept that also includes integrating a variety of values, beliefs, experiences, and worldviews. A simple example is a willingness to diversify our use of art, literature, film, music, fields of study, and more to support our points.

For example, I once showed a scene from *Harry Potter and the Sorcerer's Stone*[5] during a sermon to make a point about discernment and how, when God is calling us to follow, God will pester us until we do. In this scene, the titular character, Harry Potter, receives an invitation, delivered by owl, to attend Hogwarts School of Witchcraft and Wizardry. His uncle, a normal man who is vehemently against wizards and magic, snatches the invitation away. The next day, more owls land on the roof, and more letters slide through the mail slot.

The uncle nails a piece of wood over the slot, blocking it. Eventually, on Sunday (which the uncle cheerily proclaims to be the *best* day because the post isn't delivered on Sundays), the house begins to rumble. Suddenly, an overabundance of invitations flies out from the fireplace, through open windows, and from the now unblocked slot. I used this film, cherished by many who have tuned church out, to tune them back in. I was criticized in my town when word got out that (gasp!) I had shown that satanic *Harry Potter* movie in church, but visitors and younger members loved it. I used the perspective of something they loved and identified with to help them understand how to listen for God.

Preaching with diversity means that I am willing to use a variety of means and perspectives to help my listeners understand a Christian one. Still, if we don't help them *prioritize perspectives*, then we just make everything we offer relative and open to deconstruction. Postmodern preaching from a Christian perspective doesn't mean simply presenting our perspective as one among a number of equal options. In the example above, I used something people loved to help them more deeply understand the Christian call to practice prayer and discernment. Ultimately, we aren't trying to demonstrate how Christianity is right and everything else is wrong. We're trying to show them how commitment to a Christian path leads to a more consonant and compassionate life. We do that by exploring other perspectives, perhaps showing how Christianity is similar to them, and then taking listeners a step further by pushing them to become more open to the Christian perspective and its teachings and practices.

Another example can be found in the growing interest in mindfulness and meditation. There are *some* Christians who rail against meditation, proclaiming it to be evil because it comes from Buddhism, but that's a shrinking population. We can integrate mindfulness and meditation into our sermons by explaining what meditation and mindfulness are—how meditation is purposeful emptiness practiced to become centered in and with everything, while mindfulness is a careful awareness of oneself (one's reactions, impulses, and beliefs) and the sensations and experiences of everything around us. We can then discuss how Christians have practiced the same concepts since Christianity's earliest days, but we've called them "contemplation" and "awareness." Then distinguish between the two. Mindfulness and meditation help us become more sensitive and centered in the world around us. Contemplation and awareness do the same thing, but they also make us awake and aware of how God is present with and in and through everything. They aren't practices that merely open us up to the world around us, but they help us become aware of God's presence in and through everything. We don't denigrate Buddhism. We explore how Christianity and Buddhism may intersect while also pointing out how they diverge, with the Christian practice prioritizing the personal experiences of the presence of God rather than just stillness and attentiveness. Being postmodern doesn't mean believing that everything is relative and therefore equivalent. It means recognizing the validity of a variety of perspectives while also searching for perspectives that help us transcend mere common perceptions without obliterating other perspectives.

Finally, preaching to postmoderns requires *emphasizing experience*, the most powerful teacher. I've come to believe that contrary to our modernist belief that rational, theological arguments matter most, what makes someone a Christian is the spiritual experience of God that leads her or him to seek a deeper theological understanding and religious engagement.

Going back to the *Harry Potter* example, I was tapping into a shared experience so many in our culture have had—being fans of the books and films. I used the clip to engage them in an experience.

I'll talk much more about this in future chapters, but the more experiential we can make our sermons, the more powerful they will be. Fortunately, there are many ways to do this—through the use of PowerPoint-like slides, film clips, skits, physically engaging exercises, stories, and more.

For example, in one sermon about denying ourselves, picking up our crosses, and following Christ, I had people recite at the end of the sermon a litany capturing the theme and then had them come forward to pick up small quartz crosses to keep in their pockets. Years later members told me that they still carried those crosses every day in their pockets.

Another time I talked about how we can experience God if we're aware. Then I invited a member to come up and tell a story of her amazing experience of God, which afterward I then reflected upon. Still another time I asked members to make short videos, which I then used in sermons. The key is that we should look for ways to create experiences within the sermons while also talking about experiences.

Conclusion

I want to end with an annotated sermon that I preached in 2006 that I believe captures what I've been emphasizing. The key to preaching in a postmodern age is to do so in a way that validates instead of denigrates, that invites rather than dictates, and that encourages consideration rather than demanding compliance. Few in our present age will accept what we say simply because we are a seminary-trained, denominationally ordained authority. In an age when all authority is suspect, our authority can work against us as people look upon us as educated "elites." While offering rational arguments, teaching doctrine, and engaging in apologetics worked in an age of Christendom, when Christian perspectives were the dominant ones, that's no longer true. Our beliefs compete with so many others in our culture today. So we have to be able to engage these other beliefs and perspectives.

What's the alternative? It is understanding other people's perspectives while inviting them to consider and engage with ours. The following sermon is an example of this approach, with annotated comments bracketed and in italics.

Seeking Wisdom

Matthew 2:1-12

January 8, 2006

Do you like mysteries? I do. I'm not a great fan of mystery novels, but I am of mystery television shows. For instance, I like all of the *CSI* shows: the original one, *CSI: Miami*, and *CSI: NY*. *[I'm starting with the common experience of watching popular television shows of the time, which connects my experiences with listeners'.]* Why do we like them so much? They're surprising. You witness the crime in the beginning, but you don't know who did it or why. You then follow the characters as they piece together the murder puzzle, eventually solving it within the last five minutes of the show.

Mysteries grab us. I think we're genetically built *[I'm offering a biological, psychological point of view.]* to solve problems and overcome challenges. Mysteries appeal to our need to understand and figure out the unknown. Humans have always explored mysteries, whether we're talking about unexplored lands, outer space, the human mind, or who killed that person. *[I'm commenting on a historical point of view.]* For instance, why are the *Harry Potter* books such a phenomenon? *[I'm engaging popular culture and validating people who love the books and films while simultaneously being unlike those rigid "Christians" they see on television who criticize the books and films for being about magic.]* On the surface they may seem like books about magic, but at their core, they are mysteries. Trouble brews, and it is left up to Harry Potter and his two friends, Hermione Granger and Ron Weasley, to solve the mystery and right injustices.

Love of mystery has also made *The Da Vinci Code* popular. *[Again, I'm engaging 2006 popular culture, especially in the face of Christians who denigrated the novel and the novel that denigrated Christianity, with both setting up an "us vs. them" narrative.]* It is a fun mystery novel. The way it's written is very clever. Each chapter is no more than three to five pages long, and each chapter ends with a mystery that isn't resolved or addressed until several chapters later, but at that point, a new mystery is presented. As a book of religion and history, which some people want to turn it into, it is pure fiction. *[I'm validating the enjoyment of the novel while also calling into question the novel's historical and religious flaws.]*

Years before the book came out, I actually studied many of the biblical and religious ideas that Dan Brown uses as the foundation of the book. I had enough training in religious history and the Bible to be able to recognize its flimsy biblical and historical evidence. *[I'm now showing that I'm not just a reactionary Christian but one who has taken seriously the novel's religious underpinnings.]* It is bad religion but great mystery. *[I have prioritized perspectives, allowing them to hold on to the "enjoyment of a mystery" perspective while calling into question its perspective on religious truth.]*

Our need to solve and overcome mysteries is what's led us to explore all the continents, the oceans, outer space, and the microscopic world. *[I'm validating the yearning to learn and discussing it from a biological/psychological perspective.]* People don't like the fact that there might be unknown, mysterious regions anywhere, so we explore to discover what's out there.

Universities are a testimony to our need to solve life's mysteries. Universities and colleges train people to explore and solve the great mysteries of life. Biology departments uncover the secrets of physical life. Chemistry departments solve the mysteries of chemical life. Physics departments plumb the mysteries of the universe. Psychology departments explore the mysteries of the human mind. *[I've engaged many disciplines, showing that I value different perspectives but won't necessarily make them subservient to Christianity.]* We simply cannot stand unsolved mysteries, so we create whole disciplines to explore them in various fields.

We love solving mysteries, but our obsession with needing clear, concrete answers can become an obstacle to spiritual growth. Our passage for today is an unsolved mystery that can distract people from its deeper meaning. *[I'm now about to open them to a new, spiritual, mythological perspective that transcends the historical one.]* It's one of the biggest unsolved mysteries of all time: Who were the three wise men who visited the baby Jesus?

I'll help you with the mystery if you'll join me in exploring its deeper meaning. Let's start with the basics. We call them the "three wise men" or sing about them as the "three kings," but the Bible never says that there were three of them, nor do we even know that they were men. The original term used for them was *magi*. Magi were Persian priests in Zoroastrianism who studied the stars. *[I'm giving them historical perspective by introducing them to the Zoroastrian religion.]* They embraced ancient astrology, believing that the stars could reveal the answers to life's mysteries. In Jesus's day, they were seen as mystical figures from afar who some thought could peer into the deep secrets of life. We also know that some of the magi in Persia were women, so among this delegation of magi, one or more may have very well been women. *[I am engaging them in a biblical perspective without denigrating other perspectives, but I'm also validating that women may have been a bigger part of the story than suspected.]*

We also don't know much about this mysterious star they followed. Was it really a star? Biblical scholars, as well as others, have tried to explain what it was. *[I'm pointing them to a scientific, cosmological perspective.]* In fact, every year at this time, new television shows purport to solve the mystery of the star, even if at the end of these programs they end up saying, "So what was the star? We don't know." I've seen some pretty silly ones suggesting that the star was some sort of alien spacecraft revealing where Jesus was because he was really an alien. *[Again, I'm engaging pop culture by referencing shows many would have watched and wondered about—and I'm slowly building the priority of a Christian perspective without denigrating others.]*

What do the serious scholars think the star was? *[I'm now making biblical scholars the authority and inviting listeners to trust biblical scholarship. And you'll note that I emphasize that these scholars integrate science in their pursuit of understanding.]* Looking at the passage biblically, historically, and scientifically, they suggest that if Jesus was really born in 11 BCE, the star might have been Halley's Comet, which made an appearance then. Or if Jesus was born in 7 BCE, it might have been a conjunction of Saturn and Jupiter, which was particularly bright in the sky during that year.

The best conclusion of scholars and scientists—the one that adopts the perspective of the Zoroastrian religion of the magi—is that what they saw was a configuration of Jupiter, Saturn, and a star called Regulus, or the "king star." *[At this point, I projected a slide showing the conjunction of the planets and stars.]* It would have come together in the constellation of Leo, which the magi considered to be a royal constellation. This configuration, coming together in the early evening for weeks on end, would have been very bright, and Regulus would have seemed to travel westward out of the configuration. Scientists who have studied the stars using computer mapping have noted that this configuration occurred in 4 BCE, which is the year most scholars believe Jesus was born. This explanation also fits history, science, the Bible, and how the magi's religion operated. We can stubbornly insist they followed a moving star that settled over Bethlehem *[I'm actually joining them in their skepticism.]*, but that would have been just as weird a sight for them as it would be for us today. They would no more have followed a strange floating orb for weeks on end than we would. This configuration of Regulus would have been deeply significant to the magi, though, because in their faith, it signaled the birth of a great king.

I've helped you with this particular mystery, but there's more to this passage than the mystery. If we get stuck on that mystery, we miss the deeper point of the passage. *[I've been engaging them with the idea of mystery and am now shifting the perspective from a material one to a spiritual one—with an emphasis that while worldly mysteries are fun to solve, obsession with them can keep us from going deeper.]* We can get so focused on the mystery of the passage that we never take the time to consider what the passage is revealing. And this passage has a powerful point, a point that the Gospels tell over and over. *[I'm now offering a contrasting spiritual perspective by telling them that there's something more to consider that goes beyond a purely historical/scientific perspective. I'm opening them up to a new, spiritual exploration of the passage.]*

What's the point? The point is that we always think we know how God is going to do things, and God always surprises us by doing things God's way, not the human way. *[This is encouraging them to relinquish a purely material perspective for a more paradoxical, spiritual one.]* So many Christians think that they have the ability to figure out just how God works, and yet God always surprises us by doing things differently: fulfilling prophecies in unexpected ways, answering prayers in unforeseen ways, and intervening in life in unanticipated ways. If you look at the way God does things in the Gospels, you'll see what I mean. *[I'm pushing them to engage the spiritual point of view.]*

For instance, in the age of the prophets, God promises that the Messiah will come soon, but then God delivers on that promise five hundred years later. The religious experts of Israel believe the Messiah will be born to a powerful, influential family descended from David—a family that will be able to rise up and overcome the Greek or Roman Empires. Instead, he is born to an insignificant, unwed fourteen- or fifteen-year-old girl (who may have been related to David). That's scandalous to the experts of the time. They expect the Messiah to transform the world through the use of political and military force. Instead he transforms the world through healing and love. They expect a warrior king who smites his enemies. Instead he's a Messiah who transforms the world by willingly sacrificing himself on a cross, only to be surprisingly resurrected. *[I'm using the certitude of those in the past, incorrect as it was, to invite them to question their own certitude and in so doing open themselves to a new perspective.]*

What's surprising is that in the end, God's way is always better. Empires rise and fall, but over the course of two thousand years, Christianity has continued to grow. The priests and wise ones of Israel think that they will recognize the Messiah when he comes, but in the end, it's the pagan magi, as well as ignorant shepherds, who recognize him. *[I'm joining listeners in their skepticism about authority while emphasizing that the experience of God doesn't require great theological and academic study.]*

It's not just back then that the insignificant recognized Jesus's hand while the righteous were blind. It happens today too. The righteous think they know, but it's the humble who discover how God really works. *[I'm inviting them to become the humble who recognize God working in their lives by deconstructing a bit the authority of those who adopt a purely rational, scientific worldview while rejecting a religious one.]*

I was reminded of this last week after reading comments by the popular televangelist Pat Robertson. I don't mean to pick on Brother Pat, but he makes himself such a wonderful target with his self-righteous comments. *[I am separating myself from a person they might see as an avatar of typical Christian belief, showing that I am not like those they see on television. In the process, I'm inviting them to see me as an alternative voice and perspective.]* This past week he proclaimed that Israeli Prime Minister Ariel Sharon suffered a cerebral hemorrhage because he allowed the Palestinians to begin the process of creating their own homeland. He implied that God was punishing Sharon for dividing Israel. This isn't the first time he has made these kinds of proclamations. He suggested that back in 1995, Israeli Prime Minister Yitzhak Rabin was assassinated as divine retribution for signing the Oslo peace accords. Thus, the God of peace apparently hates peace.

I know that Robertson has probably memorized the Bible, but has he read it? If he had, he would realize that this isn't the way God works. *[Again, I'm offering an alternative religious perspective by associating myself with those on the verge of rejecting Christianity because of its bigotry while simultaneously inviting them to consider a different kind of Christianity.]* The God Christ revealed is not one of divine retribution but one of love, redemption, and reconciliation. Sadly, Robertson is like the priests of ancient Israel. He knows the Scriptures enough to be dangerous but not enough to truly see God's hand at work. He doesn't see the possibility that peace, not power, is God's way. Robertson is not a man who likes mystery. He's a man who will create certainty, especially if there is none.

You can get caught up in the mystery of our passage this morning, trying to figure out what the star was, who the magi were, and stuff like that. But if you do so, you'll ironically end up like the righteous of Israel. You'll get so caught up in trying to figure things out that you'll miss what God is actually doing in our midst. The truth is that God is always at work in the world, but God is at work in God's way, not ours. The only way we can get God to work in our way is to make our way God's way. *[I've invited people to integrate the spiritual perspective into their thinking and lives.]* That's when we see God's hand: when we are willing to give up our blinders in order to begin to see the world through God's wisdom.

I guess the question to reflect on is, What's more important to you, figuring out the mysteries of the Bible or being aware of the mysterious God when God is present among us and acts in providential ways? Amen.

CHAPTER 4

PREACHING TO ZILLENNIALS

When I became pastor of Calvin Presbyterian Church in 1996, I recognized a potential problem that could undermine me as a leader. I believed I could help the church grow spiritually, missionally, and numerically, but I knew an issue was looming not only for my church but for all mainline churches. Could we reach and preach to different generations, especially younger ones that weren't yet alive?

There were reasons for me to be confident about growing the church. I had previously served as an associate pastor in an active, growing church and was mentored by a tremendous pastor, so I knew how to lead a mainline church to be active and grow. Also, having recently graduated with a PhD in spiritual formation, I had clear ideas on how to lead a church to become deeper and more vibrant spiritually. Still, I was anxious because I knew a significant reason churches were experiencing a slow, steady drain was that younger generations were walking away. And it was going to get worse over time.

I knew that Generation X was different from baby boomers and that this generation's members were increasingly walking away from the church, exacerbating the melting away of members that had begun with the boomers. This truth was forcing churches to make what felt like a Faustian bargain: keep the older generations happy and watch younger generations increasingly walk away or reach out to younger generations and live with the unending criticism of older members as they punish us with decreasing contributions—contributions that were keeping the church alive.

In my experience, the generations previous to mine (I was born on the cusp between baby boomers and Gen Xers—does that make me a boom X?) wanted stability and tradition. Baby boomers increasingly wanted music and styles that resonated with their own tastes—or at least something less plodding and organ oriented. This led to the growth of contemporary Christian worship music, which mirrored rock concerts (the spiritual touchstone of the Woodstock generation). Who knew what Gen Xers wanted? They were leaving the church in droves and were baffling the culture at large. The churches that were good at reaching them created coffee shop–like churches (the spiritual touchstone of the Starbucks generation). The younger generations that would become the millennials and Generation Z, or zillennials, either had just recently been born or hadn't been born yet. How would we plan for them?

Looking for resources, I came across a book that changed my life and ministry: *Generations* by William Strauss and Neil Howe.[1] Rarely have I read anything that so transformed my understanding of the church—past, present, and future—despite the fact that it's not about church. Their description of past and present generations was incredibly insightful, but their read of the future was transforming, even if it was at odds with what others were predicting about the future in the mid-1990s.

I eagerly read this 538-page book for insight, and it immediately impacted how our church operated. For instance, as we were preparing to embark on a major sanctuary renovation in 1998, I had our music/youth director, Bruce Smith, read the book. Together we discussed how to shape the future of Calvin Presbyterian Church by integrating the insights of *Generations* into our renovations. There were issues to consider. First, we recognized that the churches best suited to reach out to unchurched baby boomers were conservative, nondenominational, contemporary churches and not traditional ones like ours. As mentioned above, they created worship structured like a rock concert, but they also offered an individualistic, ideological theology that matched this increasingly conservative and libertarian cohort. We also recognized that the Gen Xers would most likely reject religion in general because of their individualistic yet skeptical nature. The churches that might attract them were smaller, quirkier ones requiring less personal and financial commitment because of their anti-institutional stances toward American life. So we decided to influence the renovations (and the church) in a way that would position us to be attractive to *some* boomers and Gen Xers who were more outliers within their generations but that would eventually help us attract millennials and subsequent generations ten to fifteen years later. After we trained the design task force in these ideas, they put together a sanctuary renovation plan that had a classical look but included colors, art, and contemporary elements in sound, lighting, and eventually projection—all that would eventually be attractive to millennials. Accompanying this was a strategy for music that would include the integration of contemporary songs as well as gospel, blues, jazz, Hispanic, and even popular secular music.

Our projections were putting a lot of faith in Strauss and Howe's insights. We were rewarded ten years later as we began experiencing a significant increase in the number of single and married millennials who joined Calvin. For example, over the last three years of my ministry at Calvin Presbyterian Church, I did more baptisms than I had in the previous twelve.

We didn't ignore our older generations. We simply emphasized that we were now a multigenerational church that was seeking to have members of all ages. We were striving to be multigenerational in an era when churches were becoming increasingly monogenerational—either retaining a traditional style focused on maintaining older member support that bored and drove away younger members or adopting a contemporary style that attracted younger members but left older members feeling ignored and neglected.

Reading *Generations* as well as Strauss and Howe's subsequent books on generations allowed me to be intentional in my preaching about what generation I was targeting with any concept, story, or phrasing. Sometimes my sermons would target boomers. Sometimes Xers. Sometimes millennials. Over the past ten years, I've also been able to preach to Gen Zers in a way that addresses their yearnings.

What solidified for me how perceptive Strauss and Howe's generational theories were was the accuracy of their predictions for the early decades of the 2000s from their 1997 book, *The Fourth Turning*.[2] They made predictions that seemed unrealistic to me at the time but that have largely come to pass. They weren't futurists trying to peer into the future. They were historians who believed that history is cyclical. In other words, history never quite repeats itself, but it does rhyme and have rhythms. It is cyclical like the seasons—no two winters are exactly alike, but they're both clearly winter.

Their most fundamental prediction was that as the early 2000s progressed, America would enter into what they called a great "unraveling." This is a period when our whole culture would feel as though it was coming apart at the seams, with the real danger that we could move into a more authoritarian government if we couldn't navigate this unraveling. Reading their predictions in 1998, I was very skeptical. Yes, America was at odds, having just gone through the Clinton impeachments and the great Republican/Democrat budget debates. Still, the Cold War had ended, the Berlin Wall had fallen, ties between America and the European Union were strengthening,

China was becoming a full-fledged economic partner with America, and so much looked hopeful and unifying. They were predicting that a significant, society-tearing crisis or series of crises would occur that would be reminiscent of the crises of the Revolutionary War, the Civil War, and the Great Depression / World War II. Whatever the coming crisis might be, it threatened to tear the nation apart, thus setting the context for a more authoritarian government. Here are some of the things they predicted for the first two decades of the 2000s:

- *Economic distress*, with public debt in default, entitlement trust funds in bankruptcy, mounting poverty and unemployment, trade wars, collapsing financial markets, and hyperinflation (or deflation)
- *Social distress*, with violence fueled by class, race, nativism, or religion and abetted by armed gangs, underground militias, and mercenaries hired by walled communities
- *Cultural distress*, with the media plunging into a dizzying decay and pressures to impose some forms of state censorship
- *Technological distress*, with cryptoanarchy, high-tech oligarchy, and biogenetic chaos
- *Ecological distress*, with atmospheric damage, energy or water shortages, and new diseases
- *Political distress*, with institutional collapse, open tax revolts, one-party hegemony, major constitutional changes, threats of secessionism, authoritarianism, and altered national borders
- *Military distress*, with war against terrorists or foreign regimes equipped with weapons of mass destruction[3]

Not every one of these predictions took place in the ways they described, but there has been enough accuracy for me to give them credit for understanding the future based on their cyclical understanding of the past. Whether in the United States or other countries such as Hungary, Poland, Turkey, China, Russia, and others, we have seen an increase in authoritarian regimes, assaults on the free press, the Great Recession, long-term wars in Iraq and Afghanistan, increasing economic inequality, a significant rise in religious and domestic terrorism, climate change, and more.

A Cycle of Generations

It is quite common and normal for each generation to be irritated by preceding generations (think of the boomer declaration to not trust anyone over thirty and the now popular phrase among Gen Zers, "OK, boomer!"). It's also common and normal for them to be baffled by succeeding generations, as reflected in this statement by an elder describing younger generations, saying that they "now love luxury; they have bad manners, contempt for authority; they show disrespect for elders and love chatter in place of exercise. Children are now tyrants, not the servants of their households. They no longer rise when elders enter the room. They contradict their parents, chatter before company, gobble up dainties at the table, cross their legs, and tyrannize their teachers."[4] You may have read this quote before. It's from Socrates, who lived in ancient Athens from 469 to 399 BCE.

What makes prediction difficult is that we have a tendency to think of the movement from the past to the future as a linear progression. We think that once something is ensconced in our culture, it will last into the future, only more so. Strauss and Howe say that this is a flawed understanding of history because it doesn't take into consideration the psychology of a generation and how they've been shaped by their experiences. Simply put, each generation isn't an extension of previous generations. They are a response to and reaction against previous generations. We may have traits of our parents and grandparents, but we experience life events differently, often feeling as though we have to fix the excesses and mistakes of previous generations.

Understanding each generation's experiences and reactions, especially to common crises, helps us understand how they've shaped their cohort's approach to the world. Each generational cohort (born roughly over an eighteen- to twenty-year span) experiences shared events differently from previous and subsequent generations because they face them at different life phases. Think about the generations alive during World War II. If you were part of the eldest generations, you sacrificed comforts and offered encouragement in support of those fighting the war. If you were a middle-aged man or woman, you might be an officer overseeing war efforts, an executive managing a business supporting war efforts, or a volunteer raising funds and engaging in activities that supported soldiers. If you were a young adult man or woman, you were probably serving in the military, working in a factory, or offering tangible support of some kind. If you were a child, you were probably doing your best to be seen but not heard so as not to distract your parents and grandparents, who were busy fighting for world freedom. Each cohort's experiences shaped them uniquely.

Today, each generation has experienced terrorism, mass shootings, the Covid-19 pandemic, economic turmoil, polarized politics, climate change, and social protests differently. Simply put, they see the world, the nation, religion, science, social issues, racial issues, and life in general differently from their predecessors. Preach to a Gen Zer as we would a boomer, and we will lose her or him—as we already mostly have.

Strauss and Howe believe we have been progressing through a reduplicating generational cycle in North America (and possibly all of Western culture) since at least 1584. Thus, if we look back at eighty-year (four-generation) intervals, we will see the culture going through similar experiences. So, for example, if we look back over the past 240 years of American life, we will see a cycle of society-tearing events repeated *roughly* 80 years apart:

- 1776–82: the American Revolution
- 1860–64: the Civil War
- 1930–45: the Great Depression and World War II
- 2001–22: 9/11, the Great Recession, the Covid-19 pandemic, the great "unraveling" (or polarization)

These are the four great crises of American history. Certainly, there have been other significant crises, but not ones that have shaken America to the core as these have. For Strauss and Howe, it's not a mystery why these crises occurred. The same generational configuration existed in each: a dominant individualistic/idealistic generation aided by an individualistic/skeptical generation leading in ways that create the conditions for the crisis by tearing down stabilizing institutions, glorifying individualism and individual rights, demanding ideological and theological purity, and asserting dominance over others while the two youngest generations powerlessly act as foot soldiers and/or victims of the crisis.

Strauss and Howe tell us that prior to each of these great crises, there was a rise in an individualistic, evangelical religion and a coinciding diminishment of mainline-style Christianity. Why? Because that same individualistic/idealistic generation that leads us into an eventual crisis was a spiritually hungry generation in youth to midadulthood who sought greater personal spiritual experiences. In effect, they created a very individualistic brand of religion that was in direct contrast to the more communitarian focus of traditional, mainline religion.

Thus, if you look at the history of American Christianity, you will find that all of America's four spiritual Great Awakenings preceded a great crisis by about twenty years.[5] The first Great Awakening lasted roughly from 1734 to 1743 (although like preceding and following awakenings, the effects persist much longer). It featured fire-and-brimstone preachers such as Jonathan Edwards and George White-field. The Second Great Awakening took place throughout the second and third decades of the 1800s. It also coincided with the transcendentalist movement of the 1830s and the 1840s, which is why the authors call this the Transcendental Awakening. A Third Great Awakening, which they call the Missionary Awakening, took place in the late 1800s to early 1900s and gave rise both to the spread of Western society's missionary zeal throughout Africa and Asia and to the Pentecostal movement beginning with the Azusa Street Revival in 1906. Finally, we can potentially identify a Fourth Great Awakening, what they call the Boomer Awakening, beginning with the Summer of Love in 1967 that sparked both the eventual New Age and the evangelical movements of the 1980s and 1990s, both of which are still with us, even if they have declined from their peaks in the early 2000s (declining does not mean weakened, and the worldviews of both have an influence on contemporary events). Again, the commonality with all of them is that *an idealistic, individualistic generation dominates the culture and sparks a spiritual movement and eventual cultural crisis.*

The Present Cycle of Generations

To understand our present cycle of generations—and specifically how to preach to both millennials and Generation Z—it helps to further understand each generation so that we know how to speak to their yearnings. What makes each generation a generational cohort is that they share cultural experiences in roughly the same life stages—as youth, young adults, midlifers, or elders. Their shared experiences, reactions to previous and subsequent generations, and shared perspectives bind them in a cohort, despite the reality of outliers—those who share the same experiences but react and respond in different ways. Strauss and Howe believe that each of the historical, four-generational cohorts can be described according to four enduring archetypes: prophet, nomad, hero, and artist. The archetype conforms to the generation's general way of interacting with the world. Using our present generational configuration, here are the basic descriptions of each generational cohort:[6]

- *Prophet (individualistic/idealistic) generation (baby boomers).* They are a dominant generation (meaning that they dominate the culture in every life phase because of their sheer population size) that approaches the world in individualistic and idealistic ways, seeing the world in terms of absolute rights and wrongs. They grow up as indulged youths in the decades following a traumatic secular crisis (American Revolution, Civil War, Great Depression / World War II). As late youth / younger adults, they spark a spiritual awakening as they pursue a more idealistic life than their parents and grandparents. They become more individualistic and narcissistic as young adults, moralistic as midlifers, and visionary as elders. They both spark and lead through a subsequent national, secular crisis that creates conflict and division (what Strauss and Howe call a great "unraveling").
- *Nomad (individualistic/reactive) generation (Generation X).* They are a recessive generation (meaning they are a smaller cohort and are no match for the dominance of the generations before or after). They grow up as unprotected (e.g., latchkey),

criticized youth during a growing spiritual awakening. They become cynical, thrill-seeking teens; risk-taking young adults; sometimes angry, pragmatic midlifers; and reclusive elders.

- *Hero (communal/civic) generation (millennials).* They are a dominant generation who grow up as protected children after a spiritual awakening, come of age during a secular crisis (resulting in them often being on the front line—perhaps as soldiers, doctors and nurses, or workers—during a crisis such as the Revolutionary War, the Civil War, World War II, 9/11, Afghanistan and Iraq wars, the Great Recession, and the pandemic). They become heroic and achieving young adults, who move the country away from the individualism of the previous generations to focus on civic demands by rebuilding the torn-down institutions as midlifers and become busy elders attacked by the subsequent *prophet* generation.

- *Artist (communal/adaptive) generation (Generation Z).* This is a recessive generation that grows up being overprotected and even suffocated (helicoptered) children and youths during a secular crisis, which leads them to become deeply sensitive and even artistic. They become conforming young adults, negotiating and diplomatic midlifers, and sensitive elders, adapting to the needs of the prior hero generation and the subsequent prophet generation.

So how does this translate to our present generational configuration and how we preach? Using Strauss and Howe's generational cycle, the following sections are the more detailed descriptions of the four specific generations interacting in our culture today and who we have to think about in our preaching.

In reality, we have six generations interacting, but I'm going to put aside those born prior to or during the Great Depression. That will make it easier to focus on those increasingly walking away from Christianity—the new hero and artist generations. The following is a summary of these four generations. (As you read, please remember that these are descriptions of generational cohorts, and there are always exceptions to these generalities.)

Baby Boom Generation (Born 1943–60)

This prophet generation has been forcefully individualistic and idealistic. As teens they sparked a musical and spiritual renewal (interestingly led by previous artist generational members Jack Kerouac, Bob Dylan, Elvis Presley, the Beatles, and Martin Luther King Jr.) while focusing on individual experience and personal idealism. As young adults, they relinquished some of this idealism to focus on the individual pursuit of money and influence. As midlifers, they sparked the growing culture war by staking their ground on both sides of the conflict—personal responsibility and self-sufficiency on one side and universal rights and social responsibility on the other. From a religious/spiritual perspective, they have gravitated to either a Woodstock-inspired, contemporary, born-again Christianity or a personal experience–oriented, believe-what-you-want New Age spirituality (that is, if they haven't opted out of religion completely in adopting a rationalistic, secular worldview). They began the drain of the mainline church because of its emphasis on tradition and conformity to the community. They also sparked subsequent generations to look with skepticism on the "institutional church" because they don't trust institutional anything—churches, government, schools, international orders, and more.

Generation X (Born 1961–81)

The baby boom generation, for all its polarization and divisiveness, has generally been a hopeful, optimistic generation, believing that if everyone became like them, utopia is possible. Generation X has been a more deeply cynical and pessimistic nomad generation. Their darker stories, humor, and music are also more critical and crude, breaking boundaries and taboos. They've been a more conflicted and angry generation, as seen by the rise of drug use and gangs when they were in their late teen / early adult years as well as the rise of the Tea Party and a libertarian worldview in their midlife years. From a religious/spiritual perspective, they've been a much more atheistic/agnostic generation, walking away from the church amid suspicion that churchgoers on the right and left have ulterior motives. The religious movements that have managed to attract them have been either large, nondenominational churches that allow them to remain somewhat anonymous and distant or the emergent movement that created a more intimate, coffee shop / Starbucks–style worship catering to their idiosyncrasies. Mainline churches have had a very difficult time attracting this generation, and when they do, it's generally because the church has been adaptive enough to offer a variety of experiences that don't require great commitment (as well as children's programming adaptable to their schedules).

Millennial Generation (Born 1982–2001[7])

This hero generation has grown up amid the hyperindividualism, ideological polarization, and constant conflict of the previous two generations. At the same time, they grew up with managed playdates, constant group activities, group texting, and social media that allowed them to embrace community. As my own millennial daughter said a few nights ago, "My generation hates individualism! All we want is for the world to get better together." In every way, this generation is different from the preceding ones, and as a result, they are often unfairly criticized by boomers, who have always been really good at condemning previous and subsequent generations. They've grappled with the breakdown of institutions everywhere and have helplessly witnessed the rising problems of climate change, inequality, and oppression brought about by our culture's increasing divisions. They are singularly focused on how to overcome the problems created by the previous generations. Thus, they are a communally minded generation seeking cooperation and collaboration while also recognizing that at some point, they will have to rebuild a culture ripped apart by the individualism of previous generations. Thus, they are communal and civic minded.

A glimpse into their thinking can be gleaned by the teenage books and films that influenced them: the *Harry Potter*, *Hunger Games*, and *Divergent* series—all stories about teens who collaborate to overcome the individualistic destructiveness of their parents' generation. At the end of each, these youngsters are charged with rebuilding after defeating their oppressive, divided, power-manipulating elders. From a religious/spiritual perspective, this is a generation that doesn't quite know what to do with church. They've been deeply influenced by their religiously skeptical parents, who may have raised them away from Christianity and led them to become agnostic/atheistic. Thus, they tend to see Christianity through similar skeptical lenses, even if they themselves are more hopeful and positive, while still integrating religious teachings into their cultural beliefs—following the golden rule, caring for the marginalized and oppressed, and caring for creation. Churches haven't quite figured out how to reach out to them, which is where my previous church's sanctuary renovation, music, and preaching bore fruit. We experienced an influx of millennials because in 1997, we realized that this generation would be interested in *both* tradition *and* new, sacred *and* secular music, a diversity of perspectives *and* people, a community that encourages love *and* action, ideals *and* experiences, respect for Christian *and* non-Christian.

Generation Z (Born after 2001)

This generation's identity is still being formed as it enters its twenties. It is an extremely sensitive generation, having had to deal with high levels of anxiety as a result of a constant stream of crises throughout their childhood—the aftereffects of 9/11, Iraq and Afghanistan wars, the Great Recession, gun violence, climate change, political polarization, the pandemic, and social protests. They've felt helpless in the face of this constant stream of crises as well as what seems like a lifetime of struggle ahead to rebuild the culture when they don't know where to start.

Ultimately this is an adaptive generation that has had to adjust as children to so many cultural and national crises. Like millennials, they are communal, seeking collaboration and cooperation, knowing that they will have to join with millennials to rebuild society at some point, whether that's rebuilding cooperation in a divided nation, rebuilding international relationships, or just rebuilding crumbling bridges, buildings, and roads.

From a religious/spiritual perspective, they've been influenced by the religious skepticism of their largely Gen Xer parents and often have grown up with no religion or with an evangelical religion that turns them off because it ignores what they see as the world-destroying crises of climate change, racial/ethnic oppression, inequality, and polarization. Much as with millennials, the Christian world has struggled to articulate a faith that caters to them. The old ways no longer work, but what comes next isn't obvious. What is clear is that they *will not* be attracted to religion that comes across as polarized, divisive, and segregated—whether that means racially, economically, or theologically.

Something to be wary of is looking at large to midsized nondenominational churches and assuming that they're doing a good job of reaching out to millennials and Gen Zers. That isn't quite true. These churches reach a relatively small segment of them, but seeing large numbers in one or two local, large nondenominational churches can obscure the reality that there's a much larger group that's either walked away or was never there. In both mainline and evangelical churches, the now grown-up children and teens are walking away after high school graduation, if not before. Still, the vast majority of Gen Zers have been raised away from the church. Christianity and religion are foreign to them. In fact, they've grown up suspicious of all religions, especially Christianity, because of what they see as hypocrisy from church leaders who have been guilty of pedophilia, bigotry, mixing the gospel with politics, and just not practicing what they preach.

Boomer and Xer Preaching

Before we focus specifically on how to preach to the zillennials (shorthand combining millennials and Gen-Z), it's helpful to explore what kind of preaching is typically attractive to the baby boom and Generation X generations.

As I said before, not everyone who is of a particular generation is exactly in sync with that generation, but the vast majority are. For example, my perspective on life is not quite typical of a baby boomer, even though I'm technically part of that generation, having been born in its last year. I'm more an amalgamation of baby boomer, Generation X, and even millennial thinking. I have baby boomer optimism and passion for the transcendent, but I'm not particularly ideological. I am individualistic in being a free thinker, like baby boomers and Generation Xers, but I tend to be communally oriented in my leadership and approach to church and organizations. My 1995 doctoral dissertation, titled "From Individualistic to Communal Spirituality," reflects my struggle of living in between generations as I researched how to move away from individualism to create a more communal approach to spirituality—a movement that (like much of my writing) is either out of sync with my generation or decades ahead of its time. There are outliers in any generational cohort, but understanding generational commonalities helps us be more intentional in our preaching.

So what does preaching to each generation look like? Compelling baby boom generation preaching often has three facets—it is *ideological and theological* (whether in a conservative or progressive direction), proclaiming what the "right" way of thinking is. It *emphasizes personal experience* (me and Jesus) *and responsibility* (whether that be moral or ethical). Finally, it *emphasizes ideals* (often expressed in "shoulds").

Preaching that reaches Generation X tends to cater to their individualistic idiosyncrasies. Those who excel at it are pastors who have created idiosyncratic churches. For example, I've seen churches that have sought to attract men by offering hunting clubs, events at shooting ranges, and activities for avid bicyclers, Harley-Davidson riders, or runners. I've also seen ones that look like coffee shops, with dark lighting and small tables. Their preaching tends to be more pragmatically oriented on how to form better marriages, get along better with others, be more productive and prosper in business, and put the past away and live a forgiven life (especially attractive to Gen Xers who have engaged in some really risky behavior earlier in life).

Preaching to Zillennials

If we're to begin crafting messages that reach out to the millennial and Generation Z generations, we need to choose who we will preach to, or at the very least, which parts of our sermons are crafted for which generation—an important skill if we are trying to create a multigenerational church. Choosing to preach to generations who are actively and aggressively walking away requires us to craft messages to them that don't simultaneously alienate boomers and Gen Xers. That's no easy task because it means preaching to both boomers and Gen Xers, who are the last of the modernist generations, and millennials and Gen Zers, who are the first truly postmodern generations. The difference is that the first two generations tend to look for "one truth," while the latter two tend to embrace various—and sometimes conflicting—perspectives.

Thus, boomers and Gen Xers are more *either/or* in their approach to everything—you are *either* conservative *or* progressive, pro-life *or* pro-choice, for America *or* for globalism, saved *or* not saved, rational *or* superstitious, capitalist *or* socialist, for the economy *or* for the environment, and so many other polarities. Preaching that promotes an either/or, modernist perspective will not attract the younger generations. They seek an integration of various perspectives and gravitate toward preaching that helps them do this. There will always be those who gravitate toward extremes, but they'll listen to and engage other points of view as long as they provide possible solutions to perplexing problems. They yearn for authentic, hopeful preaching that binds people together. So let's take a look at what will and won't work.

What Will and Won't Work

First, apologetics and rationalistic arguments won't work particularly well except with outliers. Apologetics is a theological attempt to convert listeners through rational discourse—through linear arguments explaining why Christianity is right vis-à-vis all other faiths. It's a modernist approach attempting to offer one truth. Zillennials, being postmodern, aren't ideological. They're not going to spend time trying to figure out what's absolutely right and what's absolutely wrong because they don't believe in absolutes. They not only see shades of gray; they see rainbows of possibility. They talk to too many people with other perspectives to become confined in their worldview (my college-student daughter is an example, as she shares an apartment and friendships with students from India, Japan, Egypt, and Vietnam). Their pushback against those who demand adherence to one truth is that religion is archaic, irrational, hypocritical, reductionistic, and oppressive.

They do not want to be told what is and isn't true. They want to *experience* what's true. They won't buy what we say because we say it's true, but they will become open to our religion if we come across as being authentic, if our lives display what we're preaching (especially if we're preaching love—a zillennial value), if we invite them into something that feels deeply meaningful and inherently motivating, and if it has the potential to make the world a better place.

Just a simple example: If we try to prove the resurrection of Jesus through rational argument, we won't be convincing because from that perspective, it is an illogical impossibility. On the other hand, if we invite them to experience Christ's presence within them through acts of compassion and kindness, then there's the possibility they'll consider Christ's resurrection as a reality that's experienced rather than cognitively known. For instance, pointing out that when they feed the homeless, that special, deep sense of meaning and purpose they feel in the act isn't just the result of doing something good; it's there because it resonates with the deep presence of Christ already within them—the presence of Christ that isn't bound to time and space but lives within and beyond each of us. This is an alternative, spiritual perspective that's not rational but experiential.

Ultimately, those walking away want to know that their perspectives are valued. Sociologist and church researcher Josh Packard emphasizes the importance of valuing other perspectives in his book *Church Refugees*. He and his team of researchers focused specifically on the dechurched—those who had once been part of a church but had walked away. Through qualitative research interviews with those who've walked away, he found a number of common themes. One stood out to me as relevant to preaching. It is the issue of doctrinal and dogmatic preaching that is at the heart of apologetics. He says that the dechurched form their beliefs based on relationships and dialogue rather than on assenting to a set of doctrinal beliefs. They want relationships that lead to an experience *of* God rather than teachings about what we should believe *about* God. As he says, "In general, the dechurched see doctrine—a set understanding of who God is, what God expects of us, and how God acts—as incompatible with relationship formation and with the rest of their lives."[8] It's an obstacle because the dogmatic person demands assent to her or his worldview as a criterion for personal friendship and for a salvific relationship with Christ.

In fact, it is the ulterior motives embedded in the welcoming acts of so many church members as they try to entice and seduce people to their church and to their way of thinking and believing that significantly turn off the dechurched. As Packard says,

Our respondents also told us they'd encountered church planters, missional pastors, and on-campus religious groups who had utilized a "relationship first" model in which they were exhorted to make friends with people, gain their trust, and then invite them to church. Our respondents found these "shadow missions" abhorrent. The idea of pursuing relationships or conversations with an ulterior motive was anathema to them. They rejected the goal of shadow missions: to get people to come to God and/or the church. Our respondents preferred to simply reflect God's love to others.

Again, the dechurched value relationships and community above everything. These are the primary ways they encounter God and understand their own spirituality, develop a deeper understanding of their own faith, and put their beliefs into action. In short, they see their human relationships as an extension of their relationship with the divine.[9]

Preaching that respects different perspectives, that encourages dialogue—even if it's the dialogue of a family discussing a sermon on the drive home—and that is focused on the experience *of* God rather than the teachings *about* God invites those walking away to turn around. This means that we preachers need to come out of our theological silos and engage in dialogue with science and culture, offering messages on what unites people rather than preaching platitudes and doctrines.

Extending this idea of preaching relationally rather than dogmatically, if we preach in a way that is patently biased, zillennials will be turned off, whether that's bias against minorities, people of other religions, or those living in other countries. For instance, let's take the charged issue of Black Lives Matter. Preaching something as accepted by so many Christians as "Yes, but *all* lives matter" automatically turns off those walking away. Why? If you think like a boomer, you might be tempted to say that it's because they are young, inexperienced, and too liberal. Or that they don't care enough about the police. If you think that, you'd be wrong.

It turns them off because we've just negated and diluted what they see as a valid and important perspective. Most millennials and Gen Zers easily recognize that police lives matter *and* that all lives matter. They also see the illogic of asserting "all lives matter" by recognizing that after the Boston Marathon bombing or the Pittsburgh Tree of Life shooting, nobody said, "All cities matter." People also don't say in response to caring about disabled soldiers that "all disabled people matter," to people raising money to fight breast cancer that "fighting all cancers matters," to those making others aware of the problems of depression that "treating all mental illnesses matters," or to those promoting their own church ministries that "all churches matter." In essence, they want us to recognize distinct perspectives so that we can integrate them with others. Thus, "all lives matter" denies varieties of perspectives by denying something specific that *also* matters. If we want to preach a message that all lives matter, then we have to start by validating the specific belief that Black lives matter. Only then can we integrate other perspectives in a way that *also* asserts that "blue lives matter," "Asian lives matter," "Hispanic lives matter," "poor lives matter," and "rich lives matter" under the banner of "Love God, Love Others, Love Self." Love integrates by calling us to adopt compassion for all as a value. Saying "all lives matter" diminishes by dismissing the life experiences of African Americans.

Millennial and Generation Z preaching has to be dialogical preaching, and dialogue means looking at a topic from other people's perspectives as well as our own. We share our perspectives and beliefs, rooted in stories and shared experiences, in a way that doesn't force our view upon them. We also invite people to engage in experiences through their participation in the church community, their own service, and their own prayers, all of which help them become open to an experience with God. This is what encourages those who have walked away to consider turning around and walking back.

This issue of relational preaching versus doctrinal preaching exposes a significant issue for the Protestant movement. In many ways, during the Reformation, the Reformers fought against the "works righteousness," or orthopraxy, of the Roman Catholic Church—the idea that certain deeds can save us and get us into heaven. Declaring their independence and forging new theological foundations for the church, they also slowly substituted a new problem—"beliefs righteousness," or orthodoxy, which is an emphasis on the saving power of claiming the "right" theological beliefs, pledging fidelity to certain creeds, or amassing detailed/memorized biblical knowledge. In essence, if we don't believe in Jesus and the Bible in the right way, we're not saved. While we may assert that we're saved by the gift of grace through faith (Rom 3:21–25), we often fall prey to secretly believing that we're saved by having the "right" beliefs about God, Jesus, the Trinity, the virgin birth, the crucifixion and resurrection, abortion, homosexuality, and more. For zillennials, preaching in a way that invites them to grapple with a Christian experience and way of living is more powerful than imposing a "right" way of believing.

Central Values of Zillennials

In Josh Packard's most recent research of people between the ages of thirteen and thirty-five, he found that there were eight central values of millennials and Gen Zers: *accountability, inclusivity, authenticity, welcoming, impactfulness, relationality, growthfulness,* and *meaningfulness.*[10] I'm not going to cover all of these in relationship to preaching, but I do want to focus on five of them: inclusivity, authenticity, impactfulness, relationality, and growthfulness. These values focus on making the world a better place. Zillennials see a world divided by politics, economics, tribalism, response to climate change, race, ethnicity, gender, and more. They want to make the world better for everyone. In this way they embody the ideals of the boomer generation, but they are doing so in ways that make the ideals tangible and physical and not just ideological. Let's explore these five:

1. *Inclusivity.* What does it mean to preach inclusively? If you are part of a mainline denomination, you understand it to some extent in terms of racial and gender inclusivity. Packard is getting to something deeper. The younger generations want messages that open doors that allow for integration of different races, genders, and ethnicities without forcing them to give up their own cultural identities. In terms of how a church operates, expecting people to attend worship already knowing how and when to stand, sit, sing, speak, remain quiet, touch things, and more is a turnoff. As he says, "If a place refuses to embrace or show respect for those who seem not to conform to a more traditional set of practices and appearances, young people will connect with their sense of the sacred someplace else."[11] Musically, an inclusive approach may mean integrating all kinds of music—sacred and secular. At Calvin Presbyterian Church, we created a music program that integrated traditional, classical, meditative, jazz, blues, pop, Celtic, R & B, African, Latin, and more kinds of music.

    How does this same principle translate to preaching? Simply put, we need to preach in a way that assumes a significant percentage of the congregation is new to Christianity and that the rest are at various stages of spiritual and theological sophistication. We need to quit complaining about how biblically illiterate people are and preach as though it's exciting to learn biblical stuff for the first, third, or thirtieth time. In other words, meet people where they are rather than lament where they aren't. If we use traditional theological terms, emphasize traditional practices, and engage in churchy language because that's what we and our church members are used to, the younger generations will walk away or never come to begin with. For instance, if we preach using terms such as atonement, redemption, original sin, eschatology, soteriology, and more without explaining and exploring what they mean, they will walk away. If we use inside language such as calling a prayer a *collect*, invite people to have coffee in our *narthex*, and ask them to talk to the *sexton* if they have any cleaning needs, they will walk away. If our examples are always in-church examples that are like speaking in a family code, they will walk away. One reason that all of those nondenominational churches have done well is that they've reduced religious jargon. They call the chancel a *stage* and their musicians the *band* and use very pragmatic language in their sermons. They assume everyone is there for the first time.

2. *Authenticity.* Preaching to zillennials isn't just a matter of knowing *what* to say. It is knowing *how* to say it. I spoke about authentic preaching in previous chapters as being like talking with someone across a table at dinner or over drinks. So many mainline preachers use styles and affectations that harken back to previous "oral" ages. The cadence we use in our voices, our gestures or lack of them, or speaking with eyes riveted to a manuscript communicates "I'm a religious zombie."

Zillennials have a radar for inauthenticity, mainly because of the frauds they've witnessed among older generations of political, business, and religious leaders. Meanwhile, they watch YouTube, TikTok, and Instagram videos of people offering realistic and authentic presentations and reactions to whatever it is they're saying or doing. As Packard says, "Authenticity is characterized by the ability to be totally oneself, to be completely genuine without worrying about performing a certain way—whether that means looking, acting, or speaking in some prescribed manner."[12] They trust messages that are plainspoken and feel genuine—as though there are no hidden agendas.

Some may wonder if wearing clerical collars and robes conveys a lack of authenticity. I don't think so. A lot of younger pastors, especially female ones, are wearing them almost as a way of saying they are authentic because the religious vestments convey that they've devoted their lives to love and compassion. The irony is that a younger female pastor can wear a collar and come across as deeply genuine, while on an older male pastor, it seems like a mask hiding his real agenda.

Crafting an authentic image is important. Unfortunately, the drive in recent years by those in the contemporary church movement who spend a lot of time primping their image and crafting a certain kind of relatable "hip" look can come across as inauthentic because it feels as though they're trying too hard, thus hiding an alternative agenda. What seems to really matter is the degree to which there is a congruence between the style, liturgy, and preaching. For example, millennials will attend Orthodox and High Church Episcopal/Anglican and Lutheran services when those leading the services seem to do so in a way that feels authentic. Clearly the robes and collars are part of a sacramental approach where there's a coherence between vestments and the experience of the holy. Ultimately authenticity is subjective. So the more of what we do feels genuine rather than performance, the more we will preach authentically.

3. *Impactfulness.* What does it mean to be impactful? Aren't all sermons "impactful"? For Packard, being impactful means being socially engaging. Remember that the millennials are both

community and civic minded, while Gen Zers are communal and adaptive. Both generations will gravitate toward preaching that builds up community while demonstrating genuine compassion for the world. Packard says, "Organizations that commit to something greater than just what's expected—that insist on active engagement with key social issues—are organizations young people support. This may look like care for the earth from a faith community, or it may look like help providing childcare for single parents at a corporate work environment. . . . Engaging key social issues head-on, in addition to whatever good work, service, or product you are already providing, is a crucial part of being impactful."[13]

You might be thinking to yourself that what I'm really advocating as "impactful" is a progressive agenda. That's sort of right, but *only* in the sense that matters such as the environment, race and gender equality, and the building up of community are progressive issues *right now*. I've often said that today's conservatives are yesterday's liberals because they've adopted the practices that seemed so radical generations before, such as ridding the world of slavery or no longer wearing clothing that covers the whole body up to the ankles and wrists. Over the next ten to fifteen years, seemingly progressive issues will become more mainstream because zillennials will demand it. Even the more conservative of these generations will make them a priority. As one twenty-nine-year-old millennial Republican, Jake Hoffman, president of Tampa Bay Young Republicans, said near the end of the 2020 presidential election in explaining his support for Donald Trump alongside his concern about climate change, "Most people in our organization are environmentalists. . . . They want to see something done about it. Unfortunately, it's not something that the upper echelon of our party has listened to. . . . I'm doing what I can to try to bring it back to the ethos of Republican politics. We do a bad job of owning that entire subject matter."[14] Preaching that pragmatically addresses climate issues and legitimately uses the Bible to support them will attract zillennials. For example, emphasizing the Genesis 2 account of the first human's calling to care for the earth will resonate: "The Lord God took the man and put him in the garden of Eden to till it and keep it" (Gen 2:15). This is a call to respect and care for the earth rather than dominate it.

4. *Relationality.* Zillennials are more relational at every level than their parents' generations. While they're criticized by boomers and Gen Xers for always texting instead of calling each other, their parents don't get that this constant texting is more relational than calling on the phone, because every millennial and Gen Zer has ten or more group texts going on at the same time. They are constantly sharing memes, videos, and pictures with a circle of twenty or more people. They're also more likely to volunteer, have numerous part-time jobs, and commit to either mission or community building. They are constantly building relationships.

   Preaching that will engage them helps them build what Packard calls *bonding relationships*: "Bonding relationships are defined by reciprocity: mutual sharing, kindness that begets kindness, and a give-and-take in nearly all aspects of the connection. Bonding relationships are those foundational relationships that a person can rely on: close friends, family, or other relationships of love and trust."[15] So sharing stories, examples, and guidance on how to form healthier relationships will make a difference.

   Their emphasis on relationships emerges out of their deep concern for people of all walks of life. They are deeply repulsed by messages that create divides between people of all types. For example, while acceptance of homosexuality may seem too progressive for older conservatives, today's conservative zillennials are more accepting and much more likely to see preaching against homosexuality as bigoted. Interestingly, they might be deeply involved in an evangelical, nondenominational church that's taken a strong stance against homosexuality. They'll embrace the message that Jesus wants a deep relationship with each of us while actively tuning out the preacher as he rails against homosexuals. They just dismiss it as the preacher's blindness.

Ultimately, the key takeaway for preaching to these generations is that a relational/connectional emphasis is more important than an individualistic, moralistic emphasis. They increasingly see morality in terms of enhancing relationships and community and not necessarily in terms of personal choice and theological orthodoxy. So if you are going to preach against homosexuality, you'll have to do so in a way that says you still deeply care about gays, lesbians, and transgendered people—a difficult task when speaking to a generation that sees anything but acceptance as bigoted.

5. *Growthfulness.* Millennials and Gen Zers, highly educated generations brought up to value learning, will always resonate with preaching that emphasizes personal and communal growth. They aren't just looking for intellectual stimulation. They tend to find meaning in learning, whether that's learning for school or for daily life, as long as it is intended to help them grow personally to live better lives. They're gravitating toward lifestyles based on growth—becoming vegan, practicing meditation and yoga, exercising for health, and even fostering a spirituality unencumbered by religion. As Packard says, being

growthful is "a value that young people embrace and embody as a way of understanding that the world around them is constantly changing, and so remaining static is a liability. Keeping doors open and responding creatively to setbacks is about survival and flexibility. . . . As a value that drives people, it is rooted in a sense that one is never quite done 'becoming' who they are."[16]

Growthful preaching emphasizes helping younger generations deal with the real struggles of life they've experienced. Remember, this is a generation whose shared experiences have been disturbing ones—9/11, the Afghanistan and Iraq wars, the Great Recession, school and public shootings, polarization, the pandemic, and the election of 2020. They have had to adapt mentally, emotionally, and spiritually to a constant sense of crisis. Finding meaning and growth in the face of ongoing crises is a prominent theme among zillennials. In contrast to their boomer and Gen Xer parents, who they see as having devoted their lives to the pursuit of success and wealth, they emphasize fostering a healthy work-life balance filled with a sense of purpose and meaning. Preaching that engages themes of balance, meaning, purpose, compassion, and service makes a difference.

What Does a Zillennial Sermon Look Like?

It is difficult to clearly define what the prototypical zillennial sermon should look like, but I'll take a stab at describing it. Integrating all I've said above, here are three basic ways to think about our preaching that will engage the younger generations:

Preach with Them Rather Than to Them

I received perhaps the biggest compliment of my pastoral ministry ten years ago from a twenty-five-year-old. She said to me, "Graham, what I love about your sermons is that you don't tell us what to think. You invite us *to think*." I believe she was telling me that she was tired of sermons from pastors saying that we need to be or think a particular way in order to be saved, to be right with God, or even to be part of that church. She was saying that I invited her to consider a point of view without pressure to explore how to apply it to her life. That's intentional on my part. I don't criticize other points of view. Instead, I invite people to explore a spiritual alternative rooted in Christian tradition in a way that builds on other perspectives rather than offering a competing point of view. For example, I won't criticize Buddhism, but I will contrast it with Christianity by exploring how Christianity might offer "more." As I said in the last chapter, I may explore how a Buddhist view of meditation is similar to ours of contemplation yet how our practice emphasizes a personal, experiential relationship with God in and through everything. I'll point out how theirs sees divinity as more depersonalized and universal, while Christianity sees it as also deeply personal and intimate. The practices are similar, but the experiences they lead to can be different. Thus, our view builds on theirs rather than opposes it. I also might talk about how they believe in a universal divinity, which is akin to our understanding of the Holy Spirit, but we also believe in a highly personal God made known through Christ, whom we can experience tangibly in our own hearts, in and through others, and in our experiences of nature (especially understanding John's assertion that Christ is God *in* creation: "All things came into being through him, and without him not one thing came into being" [John 1:3]).

Call Listeners to Higher Communal Principles and Action

Zillennials will always gravitate toward preaching that emphasizes how to make a difference for people. They'll appreciate stories and examples of building Habitat for Humanity houses, creating communal gardens, cleaning a local creek or street, caring for refugees, and more. For example, I heard a stewardship sermon recently in which the pastor described a life of giving and included a GoFundMe challenge to support a mental health agency, a community outreach, and other charities. Giving to the church was part of the sermon, but it was in the context of making a difference for the world everywhere. Giving to the church is one aspect of and channel for a lifetime of generosity that supports care for—and changing—the world.

Speak Connectionally

How we preach is just as important as what we preach. If we stand behind a pulpit, looking down at our manuscripts, gripping the pulpit, and using odd cadences, zillennial visitors likely will not return. To me, TED Talks are the gold standard of authentic speaking. *Training Magazine* offers three Cs for TED Talks:[17]

- *Be conversational.* Speakers don't have lecterns, handheld notes, or other physical barriers, but they do speak using informal language along with props or pictures and lightly worded presentation slides that make their points. In other words, they seem a bit like they might be talking to us in our living rooms.
- *Be concise.* TED Talks are never longer than eighteen minutes, but that's really not the key. The key is that speakers make important, easily remembered points in simple ways that help

people capture the essential ideas for themselves and then work them into their own lives.

- *Be compelling.* Speakers are encouraged to share fresh ideas. Being fresh can be hard when we preach every week. Being fresh doesn't have to always mean being outlandishly creative. It simply means finding unique ways to explore complex themes. For instance, in a previous chapter, I shared a sermon about transformation using the example of a butterfly. That illustrates a concise use of picture and symbol to talk about a complex topic.

The reality is that zillennials are not like the boomers or Gen Xers, and preaching to them effectively and engagingly means changing how we preach and what we preach about. Perhaps we think we won't be able to make that adaptation. But keep in mind that making that adaptation is biblical. Paul emphasizes it:

To the Jews I became as a Jew, in order to win Jews. To those under the law I became as one under the law (though I myself am not under the law) so that I might win those under the law. To those outside the law I became as one outside the law (though I am not free from God's law but am under Christ's law) so that I might win those outside the law. To the weak I became weak, so that I might win the weak. I have become all things to all people, that I might by all means save some. I do it all for the sake of the gospel, so that I may share in its blessings. (1 Cor 9:20–23)

Annotated Sample Sermon

The following is an annotated sermon preached in 2016 that integrates many of the points made in this chapter.

Living in the Tension:
Changing the World by Changing Ourselves
Galatians 1:11–24
October 16, 2016

About thirty years ago, I came across a book that I've treasured ever since. It was written by a Catholic priest from India named Anthony de Mello. Spending his life in India from birth, where Christians were a distinct minority, he developed a distinctly different way of writing about the spiritual life. *[I'm already validating different perspectives by showing that he's a Christian integrating ideas from other traditions in a Christian way. I'm being "relational" and "inclusive."]* He was not a religious generalist, but he did recognize that stories from other traditions can teach Christians how to grow closer to God.

This treasured book was his *Song of the Bird*—a collection of very short stories and tales from Christian, Buddhist, Muslim, Sikh, and Hindu traditions. One story in particular really touched me. It's a story about a Sufi. Sufis are a mystical sect of Islam that we don't hear much about in the West. Over the past two decades, they've been targets of many, many terrorist attacks because they have a deeply spiritual approach to their faith and refuse to subscribe to the simplistic theology held by many fundamentalist Muslims. *[I'm subtly showing that religious tribalism exists both between and within religions, but I'm also building a bridge between them and Christians who suspect that all Muslims hate Christians.]* If you have ever heard of whirling dervishes who spin as they pray, those are Sufis. The story is about a particular Persian Sufi named Bayazid, who wrote about the spiritual life in the ninth century. In his writings, he often told stories about himself where he was the humble struggler. Here's the story:

> The Sufi Bayazid says this about himself: "I was a revolutionary when I was young and all my prayer to God was 'Lord, give me the energy to change the world.' As I approached middle age and realized that half my life was gone without my changing a single soul, I changed my prayer to 'Lord, give me the grace to change all those who come in contact with me. Just my family and friends, and I shall be satisfied.' Now that I am an old man and my days are numbered, my one prayer is, 'Lord, give me the grace to change myself.' If I had prayed for this right from the start I should not have wasted my life."[18]

What this story points out is that a *huge* component of the Christian life and spiritual growth is a willingness to change ourselves. To be an "unchanging" Christian is an oxymoron. We can't be a true Christian without constantly undergoing transformation. *[In this I'm reflecting Packard's emphasis on "growthfulness" by focusing on how personal change is a precursor to cultural change.]* The problem is that changing ourselves isn't easy. In fact, most of us resist it as much as possible.

All of us wish we could change the world—to re-create it in our own image. How many times have we said, "If only people would . . . , if only the world would . . . , if only our country would . . . , if only, if only . . ."?

I think our desire to change the world is the reason we get so passionate during presidential elections. We feel like these elections are our one opportunity to actually change the world by getting our candidate in. We become so passionate about our beliefs on how the world should be that we have a hard time listening when others challenge us. We don't want to hear what they have to say. There are several reasons for that. One is that we believe so strongly that we are right that we don't want to be challenged. Another is that if we listen deeply to what another says, we might be changed. *[I'm both dealing with listeners' own resistance to change and giving voice to their frustration with older generations who refuse to change.]*

Both of these problems were crystallized by something a friend said to me about eight years ago during a previous presidential election. She was telling me that she was going to vote for a candidate different from the one her husband was going to vote for and that he was angry with her over her vote. It was causing discord in their marriage. What struck her was her husband's final defense of his position. She asked him, "How do you know you're right about all of this?" He replied, "If you could only *feel* what I feel about the election and what I know, you would know that I am right." In other words, he was right because he "felt" right. *[I'm really emphasizing the opinionated anger that many of their parents have about politics but also sticking a thorn in those of older generations who believe they are right because they "feel" they are right.]*

Do you know who else felt—passionately—that he was absolutely right? The apostle Paul. He talked about his rightness in our passage this morning when he referred to his time as Saul, a rabbi and a Pharisee. As a Pharisee and a rabbi, he was deeply zealous in protecting Judaism from threats, and the early Christian movement was a threat. So he did his best to crush it. He was involved in the stoning of the first Christian martyr, Stephen. He also got permission from the Sanhedrin, the council of Jewish elders overseeing the temple and Jewish life in Jerusalem, to round up Christians to be put on trial. He hoped they would be imprisoned for their apostasy. He wouldn't mind if they were executed in the end. He also got permission to travel as far as Damascus, a gentile city to the north that was home to a large Jewish population, to capture Peter and the other apostles.

Paul, as Saul, was sure he was absolutely right because he *felt* right. But that didn't make him right. He reflects on that period of his life in our passage for today: "You have heard, no doubt, of my earlier life in Judaism. I was violently persecuting the church of God and was trying to destroy it. I advanced in Judaism beyond many among my people of the same age, for I was far more zealous for the traditions of my ancestors."

While traveling on the road to Damascus, he had a conversion experience of Jesus asking him why Saul was persecuting him, followed by three days of blindness. The experience transformed him from persecutor to follower of Christ. After his conversion, he was no longer the rabbi Saul who saw Christianity as a threat. He wrote this passage as Paul, a man who discovered that no matter how deeply right he felt about something that was very important to him, he had been wrong. *[Paul now becomes the epitome of the transformed person who gave up a "beliefs righteousness" perspective in order to become open to the experience of Christ.]* Paul went through a crisis that forced him both to change himself and to be changed.

Now despite what we may think, early Christianity was an attempt to reform Judaism, not replace it, and Paul considered himself a good Jew. His mission was now to fully include gentiles in the Jewish faith. *[Again, I'm emphasizing inclusivity and integration.]* He advocated allowing gentiles to join the faith without being circumcised, which for centuries had been the sign for male Jews of their covenant with God and a requirement to becoming a Jew. Paul had been changed, and as a result, he became a foundational figure in forming the Christian faith by bringing together Jewish and gentile practices and beliefs. Amazingly, Paul's influence ended up changing the world over the ensuing centuries, and it all started with self-examination.

Leading people to self-awareness is also part of what Calvin Presbyterian Church tries to do. *[I'm now setting a value for our church, a value that resonates with zillennials.]* Look at all the groups we offer and our educational programs. We have a number of groups—the Tuesday Devotional Group (which is about to read another book by de Mello, *Awareness*), the Faith Group, the Men's Group, the Faith and Family Connection, and more. They are designed to open us to how God is calling us to change. Also, many of our Sunday morning adult education classes are designed to help us understand ourselves better so we can live better. The past five Sundays, we have been studying the Enneagram, which is an ancient tool for self-understanding, so that we can grow psychologically and spiritually.

This focus on self-examination isn't just to get us to know ourselves better. It's to get us to know God better. One of the biggest problems that keep us from knowing God is the problem of "transposition." *Transposition* is a psychological term describing something that takes place in our relationships with

144

others. *[I'm purposely integrating ideas from another field, the field of psychology, which becomes "inclusive" of different perspectives.]* Too often we "transpose" onto others the feelings, perceptions, and conflicts we previously had with people we knew in our past. For example, do you ever see someone whose face you just don't like? It may be because there was someone in your past who looked like that, somebody who treated you poorly. So you transpose onto the person in your present the feelings you had toward someone different in the past.

If we had a bad boss in the past, we may transpose onto a new boss the conflicts we had with the old one. We may hear suggestions from a person we've just met as deep criticism because someone in our past criticized us harshly with a similar tone of voice. We transpose unresolved feelings and conflicts onto others. We do the same thing when it comes to God. We can transpose our own distorted feelings, thoughts, and conflicts onto God that may not actually be attributes of God.

Let me explain what I mean. Years ago, when I was working as a therapist, I had a client who was angry with God and afraid of God. As we spoke, she kept talking about how God couldn't be trusted because God could be gentle at one moment and angry the next. The further we dug into it, the more I realized that she wasn't talking about God as much as she was talking about her own father. He had been an alcoholic who vacillated between gentleness and abusiveness, often without warning. There never seemed to be a consistent pattern. She transposed onto God the Father her unresolved conflicts with her own father. Thus, in her mind, God was just like her own father—unstable and unreliable. We had to work on her seeing God as separate from her father. We didn't get there until she was willing to examine herself and to figure out where her thoughts about God ended and the reality of who God actually is began. *[In this whole example of transposition, I'm trying to help people become more self-aware by integrating personal, psychological reflection with spiritual reflection.]*

If we want to know God better, we have to learn not to transpose onto God qualities of ourselves or of others. In other words, to really know God, we have to know ourselves well enough to keep from creating God in our own image but come to know God through our experiences of God. Like the Sufi, it changes our understanding of who God really is and what God really wants from and for us. Examining ourselves, learning about ourselves, knowing about ourselves, changing ourselves is the first step in changing the world, not the other way around.

Still, as much as I cherish the story about Bayazid, he still missed something important. I think there was another level of this story, one that he could have added even later in his life, something that might have led him to pray in his old age: "Lord, help me have the courage to let you change me. If I had prayed that from the beginning, my life would have been very different."

Ultimately, the way we change the world is by changing ourselves, and we change ourselves by being willing to understand ourselves. Being willing to be changed by God opens us up to do what Mahatma Gandhi said many years ago: "Be the change that you wish to see in the world."

Amen.

CHAPTER 5

PREACHING INTELLIGENTLY

In the beginning of this book, I talked about how and why I stopped going to preaching classes while I was in seminary. I mentioned that I showed up for the first few classes and then decided to skip most, though not all, of the rest. I want to dig a bit deeper into my experiences because it says a lot about how to preach intelligently—as long as you know what it means to truly be intelligent.

I mentioned that I attended the first few classes and made the decision after that to not let that class be the main influencer of my future preaching. I still picked up a lot of good things from the class and from the books we read, but I was on a different mission. I wasn't interested in simply being a better preacher for those who were already in the church. I wanted to reach those like myself who had tuned out church. So I engaged in a homiletical, pedagogical balancing act—learn enough from the class to be able to preach in a church, learn enough from others to reach those walking away.

I turned to one of my favorite companions for enlightenment: the television. I focused on PBS and the Christian cable TV stations that broadcast mostly nondenominational, evangelical worship services. Why? Because they were particularly proficient at offering talks

and sermons that engaged people. There were two particular speakers/
preachers who I studied, notebook in hand.

The first person I studied was a motivational speaker named John
Bradshaw. Bradshaw was a particularly popular national speaker
in the late 1980s and early 1990s. He integrated insights from
counseling—especially the drug and alcohol field—to offer people
guidance on how to forge better lives. To be honest, I didn't particularly like him. I felt that he oversimplified insights from counseling
(although simplifying ideas is what great speakers do) and worked
too hard on being folksy. Then again, that's why I studied him. He
became a prolific speaker not only in public broadcasting but eventually through a whole series of videos. He was a regular guest on
daytime talk shows and cable news channels.

Bradshaw fascinated me. He generally spoke without notes while
walking back and forth across a stage, periodically stopping and looking directly at someone in the audience for emphasis. For both his live
and television audiences, it felt like he was talking personally to them.
He had a Southern accent that he used effectively to draw out words
that made them memorable. For example, he talked about Carl Jung's
concept of *individuation*, whereby we develop an identity apart from
our families of origin, calling it "in-di-*viiiiiiii*-du-A-shun," pronounc-
ing each syllable. Also, he took complex ideas and simplified them so
that someone without a graduate degree could understand them. The
popular author and speaker Brené Brown is very much a modern version of Bradshaw.

I also was taken by a television preacher who regularly appeared
on the Christian channel—Rod Parsley. He was the pastor of World
Harvest Church in Columbus, Ohio. It was a large church then. It's
become massive today. I'll be bluntly honest with you about Pastor Parsley: I couldn't stand what he said. He preached a version of

Christianity I'm emphatically opposed to. Still, I studied him because he knew how to connect with people.

Much like Bradshaw, he preached without notes while walking back and forth across a stage. The difference was that Parsley paid exquisite attention to everything about the worship services he led—the background, the colors, how the audience sat, how the music was integrated, what he wore, and more. His personal preaching style was an intentional integration of white, Pentecostal preaching and traditional African American preaching. There were times that he spoke in a growly, seductive voice, while at other times he bent over as though in deep pain—sweat dripping from his brow, one hand on a piano for support, the other holding a microphone like a soul singer crooning about a long-lost lover while musicians interspersed organ or piano chords emphasizing his words. Periodically he would punctuate his points by singing in a soulful way. He knew how to capture his audience.

Let me be clear again: I had absolutely no intention of becoming another Rod Parsley, but I had every intention of learning from him. He was preaching to an audience in the thousands, meaning that he was clearly reaching out to those who had walked away from the mainline church. I wanted to learn from him how to use my voice, my body, and aesthetics to invite people into my sermon.

I didn't have a language back then for what made these two figures so engaging, but I didn't need words to see and hear what was effective. From Bradshaw I learned that there was a way of being intellectual, relational, and physical that drew people in. From Parsley I learned that there was a way of being emotional, aesthetical, musical, and physical. Only one spoke in an intellectually intelligent way, but both were preaching and speaking in highly intelligent ways. It's just that the array of intelligences they displayed isn't always the kind appreciated in the mainline church. It's the limited range of intelligences we employ that diminishes our ability to be impactful in our preaching. Each one was preaching across multiple intelligences.

The Multiple Intelligences Revolution

At about the same time that I was studying Bradshaw and Parsley, a professor of education at Harvard was helping the world break free from the tyranny of IQ (intelligence quotient) tests. His name is Howard Gardner, the founder of the concept of *multiple intelligences*. Gardner questioned whether IQ tests adequately capture and quantify our level of intelligence. They might adequately quantify our level of *intellectual* intelligence, but what if people are intelligent, even geniuses, in other ways? Is IQ the only measure of intelligence? What about the superb athlete who can shoot, throw, catch, or dunk a ball better than anyone else alive? What about the sublime violinist whose playing heals pain and offers hope? What about the sensitive therapist who enables people to understand mysterious emotions, let go of shame, and build better lives? What about the mystery-seeking philosopher who can look inward to understand the depths of the human condition? Or the soaring writer who transports us to a completely different reality? Or an architect who designs a space that changes how we experience the world? Or a spiritually adept guide who helps us experience God's presence and guidance? IQ doesn't measure any of these, but being adept at these skills requires intelligence, doesn't it? Gardner's answer is an unqualified yes.

Gardner's theory captured what many of us already knew and experienced but didn't have language for—that we can be smart in more ways than mere intellectual intelligence. He says, "As the name indicates, I believe that human cognitive competence is better described in terms of a set of abilities, talents, or mental skills, which I call intelligences. All normal individuals possess each of these skills to some extent; individuals differ in the degree of skill and in the nature of their combination."[1] In other words, people are intelligent in many ways, so reducing intelligence to one kind severely limits our understanding of how to be intelligent in life.

His concept of multiple intelligences has huge ramifications for preaching because it suggests there is a kind of "preaching intelligence" that integrates other kinds of intelligences. Unfortunately, in the mainline church, we often diminish our intelligence by emphasizing only one or a few kinds of intelligence instead of intentionally integrating more into our preaching. I'll explore that in detail later. Before then I'd like to review the multiple intelligences Gardner has identified through his research.

In his seminal work *Frames of Mind*, Gardner identified seven different intelligences.[2] In his subsequent book *Intelligence Reframed*, he added two more.[3] Let's start with the basics. How does he define *intelligence*? He says, "An intelligence is a computational capacity—a capacity to process a certain kind of information—that originates in human biology and human psychology. . . . An intelligence entails the ability to solve problems or fashion products that are of consequence in a particular cultural setting or community. The problem-solving skill allows one to approach a situation in which a goal is to be obtained and to locate the appropriate route to that goal."[4] A summary definition might be that *we display a certain kind of intelligence any time we provide a solution or response to a situation that requires particularly creative insights relevant to the challenges posed by that situation.* This can mean making an incredibly creative play in a lacrosse game, providing a trumpet improvisation in a jazz tune, helping another person feel loved, identifying the emotional cause of self-sabotaging behavior, and more.

Some exceptional people particularly excel in one kind of intelligence, but most of us have a uniquely polyintelligent mix. In other words, we're intelligent in more ways than one, even if we don't have the highest intellectual IQs. I guess this is what people mean when they say that someone is book smart but life dumb or poor in school but great in life.

So what are the nine different kinds of intelligence Gardner identifies? They are *musical, body-kinesthetic, logical-mathematical, linguistic, spatial, interpersonal, intrapersonal, naturalist,* and *existential.* Good preaching integrates some of these. Great preaching integrates most.

You've probably noticed one kind of intelligence missing in this list. There have been many books written over the years about *emotional intelligence,* following the work of researcher Daniel Goleman. Gardner does not deny the existence of emotional intelligence, but he argues that it is really the combination of two foundational kinds of intelligence—interpersonal and intrapersonal. Any field requires a unique blend of the nine intelligences he has identified and researched. In the following sections, we'll look at each one in detail.[5]

Musical Intelligence

Musical intelligence is exactly what it sounds like. A person who is musically intelligent has a facility for appreciating and/or performing music. Some people aren't merely intelligent in this way. They're geniuses. Among the geniuses we might include Wolfgang Amadeus Mozart, Ludwig van Beethoven, Johannes Brahms, John Lennon, Paul McCartney, Stevie Wonder, Carole King, Lady Gaga, Beyoncé, Chick Corea, Herbie Hancock, Miles Davis, and so many others. We don't have to be geniuses to be musically intelligent though.

Ultimately what makes someone musically intelligent is the ability to conceive of, write, play, or perform music at a certain level of proficiency. It may seem that music and preaching are two separate spheres, but that's only because in the mainline church, we haven't typically brought musical intelligence into our preaching. Some traditions do. For instance, my wife recently tuned into the online worship service for a very large African American Baptist church in the Pittsburgh area. She noted how the pastor, as he moved toward the end of his sermon, had the church musicians integrate their playing into his sermon, emphasizing his points with organ chords. Eventually, toward the end, he was singing his points. There was a progression in his sermon from intellectual to emotional to musical.

For the rest of us, there are many ways to use our own musical intelligence in a sermon. For example, one of our guest preachers for our weekly online worship services for pastors (https://www.congregationforclergy .org), the Reverend Dr. Tracy Keenan, sang as part of her guest sermon.[6] She based her sermon on a song by the group the Roches, using the song to emphasize her points. I've preached sermons where instead of telling a story, I've had our music director sing a song while projecting the lyrics, all emphasizing the point I've made. In one sermon, I talked about how God can transform and reform anything from something corrupt into something transcendent. We played the Blind Boys of Alabama's version of "Amazing Grace," sung to the tune of the Animals' "House of the Rising Sun," which itself is based on an Old English minstrel tune from the fourteenth and fifteenth centuries. Afterward, a member of the church told me that at first, she thought I was desecrating "Amazing Grace" but that by the end of the sermon, I had powerfully made my point. She realized that God could redeem anything, transforming it into something beautiful.

Integrating music into preaching reaches those who are musically intelligent in ways that other forms of intelligence may not.

Body-Kinesthetic Intelligence

Body-kinesthetic intelligence refers to an exceptional ability in using our bodies. While body-kinesthetic intelligence is mostly associated with professional athletes, there are other professions that make use of it: actors, builders, sculptors, painters, drawers, dancers, magicians, and so many others.

As with musical intelligence, being physically intelligent doesn't mean we have to be professional. Many people communicate complex thoughts through body movement, especially since so much of our communication (more than 60 percent, according to some researchers) is nonverbal. I can communicate a lot simply through the use of my hands, my facial expressions, and the tone, loudness, and timbre of my voice—whether I use a nasal or deep-throated sound.

How we use our bodies in preaching is important. Unfortunately, many mainline preachers believe that developing a compelling constellation of body movements, hand gestures, and facial expressions for preaching is somehow manipulative. That's ignorance, not insight. I've spoken to a number of pastors who have told me that they stand behind a pulpit precisely because they don't want to distract people by moving too much. I always encourage them to change their thinking because preaching is a physical exercise. Standing motionless behind a pulpit is physical. People interpret a physical message from us whether we're active or static. Unfortunately, restricting our bodily movements can communicate that what we are saying is boring, out of touch, and unimportant, meaning that the sermon is something to be endured. It displays low body-kinesthetic intelligence and renders us as *less* effective preachers.

So many televangelist, evangelical, and Pentecostal preachers are criticized for being physically overactive when they preach, and yes, many are overactive—but they're also effective. We don't need to become televangelist preachers to integrate body-kinesthetic intelligence. We do need to think deeply about how to use our bodies intentionally in ways that effectively support our messages and teachings. This means studying the movements of those we find exceptional at using their bodies and integrating their styles into our own if they fit our personalities. It means filming ourselves and studying our own movements and gestures and seeking ways to enhance them.

For example, despite what I said above, I know some women preachers who stand behind pulpits reading off manuscripts who are incredibly effective just because of the way they emotionally use the intonation of their voices and their faces. Several I know are masters at conveying an incredible depth of emotion through the use of well-timed sighs, softened voices, emotive expressions, and more. That said, I'm a tremendous advocate for getting out from behind pulpits. I believe large pulpits, and even small lecterns, impede us physically and inhibit our ability to use our bodies in intelligent ways while preaching. Recently I was reminded of this when I asked my college-student daughter how many of her professors stand behind lecterns while teaching. She thought for a while and said, "I can think of only two, and they're my two most boring teachers."

I do certain things physically, and I believe that makes a difference in my preaching. For one thing, I virtually never—unless forced to by the style or architecture of a sanctuary—stay behind a pulpit. I know that walking while I preach, especially if I'm able to use my full body, allows me to express a point more powerfully. Sometimes I will walk into the midst of the pews or chairs when I want to emphasize a point or make it more intimate. There have been times that I've integrated dancing into my sermons, especially when telling a story. Having played college lacrosse at a high level, I've preached sermons where I've used my lacrosse stick and a ball to make a point. In others, I've thrown a Nerf football back and forth with a congregation member.

Or I've done simple things like looking skyward while talking about something transcendent; placing both hands over my heart while talking about a deep, personal, spiritual experience; or using facial gestures and body movements that express the emotion of the story I'm telling.

The more I've experimented with using my body, the more confidence I've developed in using it. The struggle is that in the mainline church, there's almost a taboo against using our bodies. I know because I bear some of the scars from the criticism of older, more traditional members who would rather I stay behind the pulpit. That's unfortunate because many in the younger generations, having grown up with more body awareness and after watching videos of speakers and performers using their bodies effectively, interpret that lack of body-kinesthetic intelligence as a sign of inauthenticity.

Logical-Mathematical Intelligence

Logical-mathematical intelligence is the one we're most used to emphasizing, and for good reason. As Gardner says, "In the gifted individual, the process of problem solving is often remarkably rapid—the successful scientist copes with many variables at once and creates numerous hypotheses that are each evaluated and then accepted or rejected in turn. The anecdote also underscores the nonverbal nature of the intelligence. A solution to a problem can be constructed before it is articulated. In fact, the solution process may be totally invisible, even to the problem solver."[7] It's this very "aha" phenomenon that enraptures us when considering logical-mathematical geniuses such as Albert Einstein. We marvel at their ability to intellectually figure out the mysteries of the world and universe. In many ways, people with high levels of intellectual intelligence mystify us the most. We can imagine ourselves possibly being great athletes, dancers, artists, and musicians, but can we imagine ourselves being great thinkers?

This kind of intelligence is also the easiest to test for, which accounts for the modern popularity of IQ, SAT, ACT, and GRE exams. The emphasis on intellectual intelligence is rooted centuries ago in the Renaissance. That age reignited intellectual curiosity in so many areas of life, and as it did, the Western world renewed a fascination with philosophy, astronomy, medicine, mathematics, geometry, theology, physics, history, and more. The Renaissance sparked the subsequent Age of Enlightenment, which placed a greater emphasis on intellectual intelligence.

The Renaissance's and Age of Enlightenment's emphasis on intellectual teaching and learning led to prioritizing intellectual preaching since the time of the Reformation. Reformers such as Luther, Calvin, Simmons, and more all embraced an intellectual-theological approach to religion as they explored biblical history and language. They gave rise to an academic tradition that uses the Bible as almost a kind of historical-theological data set from which they can draw logical, rational conclusions to existential questions. Their embrace of this kind of intelligence allowed theologians and pastors to feel qualified in comparison with other logical-mathematical intelligent fields such as engineering, medicine, government, exploration, trade, food production, and more.

Homiletical training for mainline preachers has been mostly grounded in teaching pastors to emphasize logical-mathematical intelligence (more the logic than the mathematics), both because of the legitimate insights gained through it and because of wanting to be accepted by the scientific/academic world for demonstrating empirical rigor. We're trained not just through classes in homiletics; we're trained through the numerous biblical and theological courses we've taken that have taught us an intellectual approach to religion.

Exegesis is a discipline rooted in an intellectual approach to analyzing a passage by breaking it down linguistically, structurally, historically, socially, economically, psychologically, and anthropologically in order to elucidate its compelling message. We have emphasized this kind of intelligence in preaching to the exclusion of almost all others.

Let me take a brief aside to reassure you at this point. In the past, when making points like this, I've noticed that people become defensive, feeling as though they have to defend traditional Christian thinking and practices, especially the emphasis on a logical, rational approach to biblical understanding and theological reflection. I absolutely believe that biblical exegesis and the historical-critical method are crucial parts of preaching. I am not advocating that we emphasize all other forms of intelligence while de-emphasizing the intellectual. I simply believe that intellectual intelligence is one form of intelligence, and we need to be better at balancing it with the other forms of intelligence. This means finding ways to express the intellectual *through* the use of other forms of intelligence.

The fundamental problem for those of us committed to a mostly intellectual approach to preaching is that those walking away still believe religion lacks intellectual validity. They won't be swayed by purely intellectual sermons. They will say that we try to use the Bible to justify anything, that the Bible is a book of superstition and ignorance, and that the Bible lacks objective information. So integrating other forms of intelligence invites people to listen and reflect in ways that reach more than just our cognitive minds, just as listening to a favorite song, such as Stevie Wonder's "Living for the City," might lead us to accept a compelling idea that would be ignored if it was turned into a twenty-minute lecture on racism. It's important to have a level of intellectual rigor in our sermons while simultaneously engaging those walking away through the various ways *they* are intelligent.

I won't go into detail about what logical-mathematical intelligent preaching looks like, since most of us have already been trained in it. What I will say is that the most effective preaching drawing from this kind of intelligence takes complex concepts and theologies and articulates them in simpler ways, often utilizing other kinds of intelligence. For example, I once did a sermon on the concept of predestination—a concept that people often have strong opinions about, even while deeply misunderstanding it. Most people who say they don't believe in predestination confuse it with *predetermination*—the idea that God is a puppet master orchestrating a grand marionette drama. They also have a hard time connecting it to Paul's concept of "election"—that God chooses whom God chooses (Rom 8:28–30) and bestows on them what God bestows on them.

In this sermon, I projected a map of Western Pennsylvania and Western New York on the screen. I told the congregation about a workshop I had spoken at for Lutherans in Olean, New York, the previous week. I told them that I had to drive there—that it was my *destination*. I used it as a metaphor for God calling us to a particular destination in life or the afterlife: "being saved." I then showed them the route I took, which was the shortest route. But I also said that while Olean was my destination, I had complete freedom to choose the route. I could drive along the shortest route, or I could take a more scenic route. I could choose to fly to Buffalo and rent a car. I could also choose to take a bus to Chicago, a flight to China, a train across China, hike across the Himalayas into India, hitchhike to Goa, board a ship to South Africa, motorcycle all the way up through Africa to Tripoli, sail across the Mediterranean to Rome, fly from Rome to New York, and rent a car and drive to Olean. In other words, God may choose our destiny, but we have the freedom to respond to God's call, to decide how we are to live on the way to that destiny. I then talked about how God calls us to take the best route, but we don't have to take it. We have complete freedom to choose our route, in the same way that God gives us freedom to live our lives, but God will also let us suffer the consequences resulting from the routes we take. God chooses the destination, but we choose how we will live on the way to that destiny.

I used metaphor and visuals to teach the intellectual, articulating complex concepts in a simpler, more tangible way that met people where they were by integrating other forms of intelligence.

Linguistic Intelligence

Linguistic intelligence is exactly what it sounds like—intelligence in language and writing. Novelists, poets, playwrights, and many non-fiction writers have deep intelligence in these areas. They know how to craft complex thoughts and emotions into compelling sentences, paragraphs, chapters, and stories. They write and speak in ways that compel us to read and listen.

For example, the very popular preacher Barbara Brown Taylor clearly has a deep linguistic intelligence. Other preachers are better at preaching in ways that are intellectual, physical, emotional, and the like. Yet she has a facility with words that can be stunning. I heard her speak at the National Cathedral years ago as part of an event based on Diana Butler Bass's (another author with deep linguistic intelligence) book *Christianity for the Rest of Us*, where I was a workshop presenter. My experience then and at other times is that Brown Taylor offers wisdom that's similar to other preachers, but she frequently does so with an incredibly well-crafted sentence that makes you sit up and go "Whoa!" In my experience, those sentences can be so well crafted that you almost miss the rest of the sermon as you mull them over in your mind.

The struggle with integrating linguistic intelligence into our sermons is that we need to do two things at the same time. We first need to preach in an authentic way—not reading off a manuscript—becoming more orally focused and less literary in our presentation. At the same time, we have to craft our words in a way that compels people to listen. What I've learned from preachers such as Brown Taylor isn't how to preach a sermon that's compelling for twenty minutes straight but instead to find a way to craft several sentences within a sermon that get people to sit up, listen, and contemplate. If we try to craft the whole sermon that way, listening becomes kind of like a daylong massage—eventually it gets irritating because it gets to be too much.

So using the example above about my sermon on predestination, I might talk about the different routes to get to Olean, New York, but to sum it all up, I might craft a linguistically intelligent sentence such as this: "God may be responsible for our destiny in the afterlife, but we're responsible for living into that destiny in this life."

Spatial Intelligence

Spatial intelligence is the ability to understand spaces, such as in navigation, architecture, and design. What does this kind of intelligence have to do with preaching, since there's no apparent connection with the ability to understand spaces and distances?

The answer is that when it is combined with artistic, interpersonal, and intrapersonal intelligence, it has a lot to do with aesthetics. Going back to my time of studying Rod Parsley as well as many evangelical preachers and their services, it was clear that they spend a lot of time designing their worship spaces. They spend a lot of time thinking through how these spaces open up their audience. Is it distracting? Is it facilitating? Is it too large? Is it too small? Those who practice the Chinese concept of feng shui—understanding the flow of a room or a building's environment—demonstrate that how things look and feel is important.

In preaching, as much as we have control over it, we need to pay attention to aesthetics. I think it involves both our personal aesthetics, such as how well groomed or sloppy we look, as well as public elements, such as how neat or sloppy the chancel, pulpit, and musician spaces are. I'm not a perfectionist by any stretch of the imagination, but I did have areas where I was. The worship space and sanctuary were one. I constantly worked with our musicians to ensure that their spaces—and especially electric cords and music stands—were neat and orderly. I also emphasized to our whole worship staff that what people see on Sundays impacts their worship experience. In addition, how well we use the space around us matters. Are we willing to move around the sanctuary in a purposeful way that engages people spatially, or do we stay confined to a pulpit in a way that shrinks the space around us?

Spatial intelligence is concerned with colors and art in our sanctuaries but also the slides we create for projecting Scripture, song lyrics, and backgrounds as well as the format of our bulletins. Too many pastors and leaders of churches are oblivious to the basic design principles we can use to craft effective presentation slides. When I've visited churches with fairly sophisticated projection systems, I've noted how often they'll project lyrics and Scripture with either black words on a white background or white words on a black background. They don't consider adding three-dimensional backgrounds, such as mountain or meadow vistas, clouds and skies, or pictures that go with the Scripture (e.g., a desert mountain when showing Scripture for the Sermon on the Mount, a stream for Scripture about Jesus being baptized, a garden for Scripture about Jesus praying in Gethsemane). Also, when using slides during the sermon to teach a point, are we mindful of how pictures communicate points as well as the words? Space isn't just the physical space we're in. Imaginative space can act like a window on new vistas. Adding to this, are we mindful of how our bulletins are designed? Often mainline church bulletins are crammed full of words, which in a world that is becoming less wordy and more image focused communicates that we are a church that is all about talk, talk, talk.

A final note as online worship and preaching becomes more and more important for churches: how we use space around us in our videos makes a difference. I've seen too many videos of pastors with a tight shot of their heads and a bookshelf in the background. That's poor spatial intelligence. What do we do instead? Think about how our background reflects our message. For instance, in the videos I've created as part of our online worship services for pastors, I've carefully considered and created a background to subtly communicate a message (not Zoom-style, digitally created backgrounds but real backgrounds). It may be germane to my sermon, or it just may be designed to relax and center people. It's also important to consider lighting and camera angles. For example, in one sermon preaching about the struggle to be more disciplined, I recorded myself in my home gym while talking about how hard it is to convince myself to do things that are good for me (https://www.youtube.com/watch?v= xK2YKDh8Lig). When preaching about being patient, I recorded myself sitting at a table in a local restaurant, pretending I was waiting for my daughter to show up (https://www.youtube.com/watch?v= Wrz0LmJ7M9o). When preaching about the need to emphasize relationships over rightness, I sat at a dining room table, invitingly set for dinner (https://www.youtube.com/watch?v=x9gRELnZ6zE). How we use the space around us is important.

Interpersonal Intelligence

Interpersonal intelligence is also called relational intelligence. I consider this the second most important form of intelligence for preaching, although in the mainline tradition, since we're so academically oriented, many would consider logical-mathematical intelligence to be the most important. Why do I consider interpersonal intelligence the second most important? Because preaching is primarily relational. If our listeners don't trust us, they won't hear us. If we don't engage them relationally, they won't engage us intellectually. If they don't feel a connection with us, they won't allow us to influence them.

Interpersonal intelligence in preaching also integrates many other kinds of intelligence, because making a connection with others requires us to use our bodies, our voices, the space around us, our language, and our thinking. Gardner sees interpersonal intelligence as a particular intelligence, but in preaching, it is also an integrative intelligence. Interestingly, some preachers who are well known and well cherished don't have deep interpersonal intelligence outside the pulpit, but they're deeply relational while preaching. Often they serve far more effectively in large churches, seminaries, or academia or as authors and researchers unaffiliated with a particular congregation. The point is that even if we aren't extroverts who have a natural gift for relationship building, we can still work on developing a relationally intelligent preaching style.

Focusing on how to connect with people and help them feel as though we are speaking to them personally is a crucial intelligence to develop. It's a skill that can be developed, especially working with public-speaking coaches who can help us use our voices, bodies, and composition to create a more interpersonally intelligent sermon.

Intrapersonal Intelligence

Intrapersonal intelligence is the ability to know ourselves. As Gardner says, it is knowledge of the internal aspects of a person: access to one's own feeling life, one's range of emotions, the capacity to make discriminations among these emotions and eventually to label them and to draw on them as a means of understanding and guiding one's own behavior. A person with good intrapersonal intelligence has a viable and effective model of him- or herself—one consistent with a description constructed by careful observers who know that person intimately. Since this intelligence is the most private, evidence from language, music, or some other more expressive form of intelligence is required if the observer is to detect it at work.[8]

This intelligence aids in the work of other intelligences, especially in fields such as counseling, spiritual direction, coaching, and pastoral care. It helps us know ourselves, our motivations, our baggage, and our predilections while also maintaining the ability to choose how we will be influenced by them. For example, this intelligence helps therapists gauge how we feel when a client tells us her or his problems. We can tap into our own experiences and emotions to deepen our empathy and to fully understand what the other is experiencing, which helps us sense intuitively how to respond to a client's issues.

In preaching, our own experiences are a deep source for understanding the struggles people go through spiritually and existentially. Digging into our own experience can be the difference between preaching out of the "book of platitudes" and preaching out of the "book of life." Too often I've heard sermons at funerals, for example, where a deeply personal sermon is called for, but the pastor offers one that is simply a bunch of religious platitudes strung together. Those are the ones least likely to have an impact on others and help them grieve. When we're able to dig deeply into our own struggles, confusion, successes, and failures, we become more able to address people where they are and offer insightful and compelling guidance through our sermons. That doesn't necessarily mean we have to talk about ourselves. Instead, it can mean being aware of our own struggles and how they connect with others. In the last chapter, we'll talk about preaching spiritually in depth, but doing so connects with intrapersonal intelligence. Exploring and understanding our own spiritual struggles and how we've dealt with them can be an incredible resource for teaching people how to navigate their own struggles and grow.

Naturalist Intelligence

Naturalist intelligence is the first of two kinds of intelligence that Gardner added to his list after his initial research: "Persons with a high degree of naturalist intelligence are keenly aware of how to distinguish the diverse plants, animals, mountains, or cloud configurations in their ecological niche."[9] It's the kind of intelligence possessed by a farmer, a forest ranger, a fishing guide, and anyone else has who lives in touch with nature. It took Gardner a long time to accept this kind of intelligence, but in the end, he saw that people with a special affinity for nature also have an intelligence that helps them deeply understand it from an intuitive place.

How does naturalist intelligence fit into preaching? Jesus clearly had it, as can be seen through his use of parables involving vines, sheep, crops, and the nature of animals. We express it in sermons as we demonstrate an understanding of how nature and God fit together. We use this intelligence as we develop nature metaphors and as we preach in ways that help people feel a greater sense of God through nature.

Existential Intelligence

Existential intelligence, the second intelligence Gardner added later in his research, is what I would call "spiritual" intelligence, although Gardner was reluctant to use that term. I consider this to be *the* most important intelligence for transformational preaching. He worried religious people might align this kind of intelligence with a particular theology or religious practice. He also knew that those in the scientific world, being deeply skeptical of religion, would object because spiritual intelligence could not be empirically tested and verified. So Gardner uses the term *existential intelligence*, which he associates with finding meaning and purpose in life.

He calls this "the intelligence of big questions" based on the human proclivity to ponder the most fundamental questions of existence. Why do we live? Why do we die? Where do we come from? What is going to happen to us? What is love? Why do we make war? These questions transcend perception; they concern issues that are too big or too small to be perceived by our five principal sensory systems.[10]

For a preacher, the need for this kind of intelligence is obvious. It's crucial to be able to explore big questions and offer perceptive answers to such ponderings in our preaching. I think Gardner's fear of criticism from the religious and the scientific populations caused him to hold back in exploring more thoroughly this kind of intelligence. As a result, he never really dialogued with those in the religious realm. We aren't similarly constrained. We are called to embrace deeper questions and explore transcendent dimensions. Those with spiritual yearnings for a direct encounter of the holy are eager to explore deep experiences. That's an element that's missing in Gardner's understanding. Regardless, nurturing a kind of existential intelligence is crucial for deeper preaching for reasons that seem obvious to me. Our sermons are about existence and transcendence.

Multiple Intelligences and Preaching

Great preaching requires a great integration of multiple intelligences. Identifying the particular intelligences is helpful, but the key to making our preaching excel is integrating a mix of them into our sermons in our own unique ways.

We can never integrate them all equally, but we can be intentional in how we bring them together. Looking back on John Bradshaw's talks for PBS on addiction and recovery, I see how he integrated a number of intelligences such as logical-mathematical, body-kinesthetic, linguistic, spatial, interpersonal, and existential. Rod Parsley integrated those while including musical and existential intelligence. Still, the two didn't integrate the same way even with the intelligences they held in common. Each one integrated these intelligences in unique ways.

What does an understanding of multiple intelligences in relationship to preaching teach us? First, it teaches us that those walking away respond better to insights offered through a combination of intelligences, despite those who prefer that sermons be intellectual and doctrinal. For example, over the years, I've been criticized by staid old Presbyterians (mostly from outside of my church) for walking around too much while preaching and praised by younger, new members who said it was a factor in their coming to our worship services. Second, it teaches us that if we want to enhance our preaching and reach out to those who are walking away, we have to develop intelligences in the areas where we're weak. But wait! Aren't these intelligences natural? How do we work on intelligence we may not have?

It is tempting to think that whatever intelligence we are talking about is mostly due to nature rather than nurture. For example, many who embrace the Myers–Briggs Type Indicator or the Enneagram see their fundamental categories as fixed descriptions of who we are. I don't agree. I believe these tests tell us more about what we need to work on. They tell us in what ways we may be naturally gifted, but that is not the same as saying that they describe who we are. For example, a number of years ago I was sharing a shuttle ride from a conference to the airport with other participants. As we discussed the conference and as I shared my approach to leading a church, one of the others said to me, "You must be a J!" referring to my potentially having a Myers–Briggs, "judging" personality—one that prefers to follow rules and to focus on details, plans, and structure. "Nope," I said. "I'm a P." She then challenged me and tried to convince me that I must have misread the results. I told her that whenever I take a Myers–Briggs test, I consistently test as extremely P, as having a "perceiving" personality—preferring to improvise, leave options open, be flexible and spontaneous. I thanked her profusely for her misdiagnosis and told her it was a great compliment. She cocked her head trying to understand. I told her that I am a natural P but that years before, I recognized that good leadership requires also being a strong J, and her comment meant that I had done a good job of developing a stronger J approach to leadership, providing structure, clarity, processes, and plans. In other words, I had done a good job of shoring up my personality so I could lead as *both* a P and a J, which makes for a much more adaptable leadership style.

Intelligence is both natural and shaped. We have a role in that shaping. We can choose to develop intelligence in areas that don't come naturally. I know I had to do that to become a therapist. During my long training and education, I recognized that one of my shortcomings was my background. I had grown up in a very Waspy culture, where men didn't cry or show sensitive emotion. Add to that the fact that I grew up as an athlete, where emotion other than anger or aggression is seen as a weakness. How do I become sensitive and empathetic to the pain of others when I've spent a significant part of my life repressing it?

Having recently seen the film *The Color Purple*, which is a dramatic and traumatic film about abuse, oppression, racism, and tragedy, I was clearly aware of how sad and emotional the film was yet how much I pushed down my own resonant emotions while watching it. I saw the film as an emotional training ground. I developed a plan. I proceeded to watch the movie about five times over the course of a month. Each time I sat in the second row during a matinee of a mostly empty theater. I wanted to be immersed in the film. I was determined to keep watching that film until I was able to stop pushing down my feelings and allow tears to fall. Each time I felt like crying, I could feel a mechanism within me pushing the tears down—to the point that each time, that repression gave me a sore throat. By the fourth viewing, I was able to truly tear up. By the fifth, the tears flowed easily. I've done such a good job at it that now I cry secretly through commercials and any shows that tug at the heartstrings. I say secretly because now I've become hooked on Hallmark movies. It's a joke in our family that I watch and tear up at them.

Preaching requires that same kind of willingness to work on integrating underdeveloped intelligences. For example, if we're used to standing behind a pulpit and exhibiting little body movement and facial expression, we need to develop those abilities. That means stepping out and taking risks, especially if we're uncomfortable. It means being willing to both look stupid and be criticized. It also means doing what athletes do: viewing videos of our performances, taking notes on weaknesses, and making specific plans for shoring them up while simultaneously looking for ways to stretch and grow—or maybe working with a coach. It also means watching other preachers and what they do and trying to imitate those mannerisms and affects that we think we can integrate into our own style. The point of all of this is not to become something we aren't. It is to become more effective in how we share our insights.

Everything I just said about integrating body-kinesthetic intelligence goes to integrating and enhancing all other intelligences. I have one particular superpower that most other pastors don't. I'm proud of it. What is it? I have a very attuned sense of what I don't know and a willingness to do the work and get the training to become better at it. That willingness led me from being a therapist, to being trained as a pastor, to then getting trained in spirituality and spiritual direction, to then becoming trained in leadership and organizational dynamics, to then becoming adept at teaching, training, public speaking, and more. I've spent time studying the connection between religion and science, brain structure and spirituality, visual projection technology, musical improvisation, pop culture, world and religious history, generational theory, other religions, creative writing, and much, much more. The more we move out of our silos and stretch into areas where we're lacking in intelligence, the better we are able to adapt to a rapidly changing culture, including people walking away from religion. You can see all my different interests in the development of this book. I am intentional about bringing into the art of preaching insights from areas most pastors and professors of homiletics ignore but that can be deeply helpful in revitalizing our preaching, our worship, and our congregations.

Developing Intelligent Preaching

The following exercises will help you be more purposeful in integrating multiple intelligences into your preaching. The first is a multiple intelligence reflection on a past sermon, and the second, an opportunity to construct a new one.

Reflect on a Previous Sermon

- Step 1: Choose a relatively recent sermon of yours that you liked.
- Step 2: Reread or rewatch the sermon, noting with initials or notes where you believe you adequately integrated a particular kind of intelligence (e.g., *BK* for body-kinesthetic intelligence, *L* for linguistic, *IerP* for interpersonal, *IraP* for intrapersonal, and so forth).
- Step 3: Make a note of what was lacking in your sermon, and reflect on ways you could have either integrated other intelligences or enhanced one kind of intelligence over another. Be specific.
- Step 4: Practice on your own preaching the sermon again, perhaps recording it, but this time integrating the other identified intelligences.
- Step 5: Reflect on your integration and consider concretely how you might have enhanced even that.

Construct a New Intelligent Sermon

- *Existential intelligence.* Using Scripture or another source as your guide, reflect on a theological/spiritual topic to be covered in the sermon. Hone this topic to a simple sentence, integrating both linguistic and logical-mathematical intelligence. Fine-tune the statement until it can be used as a clear guide for your sermon. For example, *If we are to experience God, we have to be intentionally receptive to God.*
- *Logical-mathematical intelligence.* Think through the logical *from-through-to* steps captured in your short statement, using the insights from chapter 2 on transformational preaching. Out

172

of that, outline a progression for the sermon that makes logical sense. For example, using the sentence above, outline parts on (1) the experience of God, (2) how ambivalent we can be about wanting that experience, and (3) how we can learn to become receptive.

- *Intrapersonal intelligence.* Reflect on your own transformation and plumb your experiences to explore the topic. What holds us back? What helps us go forward? What are personal pitfalls? How can we be either resistant or receptive? What do these experiences tell you about other people's experiences? Don't just use platitudes and religious jargon to express these ideas; use your own struggles to explore deeply what the topic means and requires. Write down your insights, and then think through how you might use them in your sermon, either to give people insight into the struggles they may well face or to offer a story of your own experiences of struggle and success.

- *Interpersonal intelligence.* Imagine yourself as another person listening to your sermon rather than thinking it through from just your own perspective. Perhaps imagine experiencing your sermon from the perspective of a church member who listens intently for theological correctness, another whose attention fades, and a third who will be critical for more personal reasons. Think through what you are saying from their perspectives, and use that as a way of articulating your ideas so that they can be more receptive to what you are saying. Develop your ideas relationally, taking into consideration how to articulate your point in a way that nurtures relationships and trust rather than demanding fidelity to your ideas because they're, well . . . right.

- *Linguistic intelligence.* With linguistic intelligence, begin writing the sermon, or at least begin crafting what you've already written, thinking through how what you say will be the most transforming. You aren't writing the next great novel, nor are you scripting the screenplay for the next great film. You are crafting a sermon linguistically that's designed to help people *hear* something that will be transforming, even if that transformation is a *barely noticeable difference*. Some of what you craft will be descriptive, some will be insightful, and some should be captivating and inspirational. The key is to think about this not from a literary perspective but from an oral perspective. In other words, if you were sitting with someone and talking about your idea, what might that person say to you that would get you to consider an alternative perspective? You might even run some of your sentences or phrases by someone, asking, "Would how I said this make a difference to you?" Remember, though, that sermons are still meant to be spoken, not read. You want them to be dialogical and conversational in tone.

- *Spatial/body-kinesthetic intelligence.* Step away from linguistically crafting the sermon and consider instead how to use your body and environment to communicate your ideas. When I first started serving at Calvin Presbyterian Church, I spent time in the sanctuary taking in the space and figuring out how to preach from it most effectively. I thought about whether to stand behind the pulpit (which limits our ability to integrate body-kinesthetic intelligence) or if I was to move away from the pulpit, how to do so. I actually practiced walking around while I preached. Initially, I placed my sermon outline both on the pulpit and on a small bookstand/lectern on the front pew. That allowed me to go back and forth between the pulpit and the congregation while still seeing my sermon outline. Over time, I became confident enough to have a copy only on the pulpit, trusting in my ability to remember without notes and to periodically improvise. Now I return to the pulpit only to refresh where I am in the sermon or to read aloud those carefully crafted sentences that were intended to be remembered. Our surrounding space and our bodies are intertwined in our preaching. The significant question is how the two interact. In an age of online preaching, spatial intelligence takes into consideration our background, the lighting, how much of our body to show, and more.

- *Musical intelligence.* As I mentioned before, music can be a tool for preaching. At times in my sermons, I've had our musicians sing a song as a point for my message. I've played an Al Green or Jars of Clay video to capture a point. I've sung lyrics to a song or played a pop song. In general, over the past one hundred years, we've gone from being a mostly verbal culture to a significantly musical culture. How we use music in preaching can be crucial and can potentially open a whole new way to connect with people. So consider how to use music in whatever sermon you're crafting. A great example of this was a sermon I preached early in my ministry at Calvin Presbyterian Church. I told the story of a young Jewish rabbi coming to a Polish community after their wise, old rabbi had died. Community members were anxious about their new, young rabbi and so peppered him with question after question upon his arrival. Instead of answering them, he began to hum a tune and slowly tap his foot. I imitated the foot tapping and had our music director slowly and quietly play the theme from *Zorba the Greek* (I realize that's not a Jewish song, but it sounds a bit Jewish and worked for the sermon). I continued the story: the rabbi started slowly at first, and then his humming and tapping grew in intensity. As I said this, I started dancing slowly in my bad version of a Jewish dance. As the song intensified, so did my dance—to the point that by the end of it, I was twirling and swinging my stole as I danced around the front, telling the members that as the rabbi danced more exuberantly, the villagers joined him in the dance. The punch line of the story is that once they were all dancing as one, the rabbi suddenly stopped. As I said this, our music director dramatically stopped the song in midphrase. I then said to the congregation, "The rabbi looked at them and asked, 'Any more questions?'" The point was that the rabbi came to give them joy and life. That was the point of my sermon too, and in telling it, I integrated musical, spatial, and body-kinesthetic intelligence. In crafting your sermon, see how you might integrate music into it as a way of enhancing creativity.

Summary

I've given you a lot of information in this chapter, and it's easy to ask the question, "OK, fine, but how do I become intellectually, physically, spatially, musically, interpersonally, intrapersonally, naturalistically, and existentially intelligent in my preaching all at once? It's too much!" You're right. In fact, I didn't even cover naturalistic intelligence in the section above, but that's because it's the one form of intelligence that we're able to cultivate only periodically, because we're in mostly fixed sanctuaries. Still, integrating all of that is a lot. But you don't have to make every sermon intelligent in all of these ways. Or more accurately, your sermon doesn't need to be equally intelligent in all of these ways. You want to integrate different intelligences in your sermons in ways that are appropriate to your topic and message. Sometimes you will craft one sermon in ways that draw more on particular kinds of intelligence and craft another sermon with a different combination. The point is to be flexible and to integrate multiple intelligences *so that your message can impact people in a variety of ways.*

Some intelligences should be integrated into your preaching more consistently. We should think about how we use our bodies and how we use the space around us. We should be existentially intelligent, since that's foundational to preaching (much more so than logical-mathematical intelligence). Other times, we can be more selective, considering how we might integrate music into our sermons or even how purposefully intellectual we are. The more multi-intelligent our sermons are, however, the more creative they will also become. Understanding multiple intelligences can help us make decisions to decrease our overreliance on one kind in order to connect with people and transform them through other kinds. We need to give ourselves permission to be polyintelligent, which leads us to be more creative. To do this, we have to be willing to stretch, grow, take risks, and practice, practice, practice.

I'll refer back to chapter 2 to simply restate that sermons are meant to be transforming. If we aren't intentional about integrating different kinds of intelligence, we will diminish the ability of our sermons to transform our listeners.

CHAPTER 6

SUCCESsFUL PREACHING

Martin Luther King Jr. is one of my spiritual heroes and mentors. He's fascinated me ever since I witnessed the shock caused by his assassination on April 4, 1968. As a nine-year-old, I overheard adults on television, on radio, and in person discuss his life and impact. Their discussions captivated me. Why was he so revered? Why were they all so upset about the death of this man I had never heard of? Why was my mother so sad about it? Why were others calling him a commie, a pinko, a fraud, and much, much worse? Who was this man, and why would someone kill him?

I asked my mother who he was and why everyone was so upset. She told me to sit down and then said (please excuse the language of the times), "He was a *great* man. He stood up for colored people, who are being discriminated against. He told the world that all people are equal and that all people are important. He made sure white people like you and me knew that colored people were just like us and needed to be treated equally. He was shot because some people hate colored people. They don't want colored people to be equal, because they are bigots and bad. Martin Luther King Jr. showed us that all are equal. This is a really, really sad thing that's happened."

In the ensuing years, I read a number of biographies and many of his books. As I've listened to his "I Have a Dream" speech over and over through the years, I've felt as though his message was just as much for me as it was for African Americans:

> I have a dream that one day this nation will rise up and live out the true meaning of its creed, "We hold these truths to be self-evident, that all men are created equal."
>
> I have a dream that one day on the red hills of Georgia, sons of former slaves and the sons of former slaveowners will be able to sit down together at the table of brotherhood.
>
> I have a dream that one day even the state of Mississippi, a state sweltering with the heat of injustice, sweltering with the heat of oppression, will be transformed into an oasis of freedom and justice.
>
> I have a dream that my four little children will one day live in a nation where they will not be judged by the color of their skin but by the content of their character.
>
> I have a dream today![1]

Why, out of all his speeches and the speeches of that era, does this one stick in our minds and souls five decades later? Why does it continue to inspire? It has an almost scriptural quality, motivating people to overcome human bigotry and tribalism—to yearn for something better. Interestingly, the actual "dream" part of the speech wasn't even part of his manuscript that day.[2] He was supposed to talk about "normalcy never again," but it felt wrong. As he stood in front of the Lincoln Memorial, King's speech soared ever higher as hundreds of thousands listened in rapt attention. He reached the apex of his speech. The next line was to call people to "normalcy never again." King paused. Mahalia Jackson, who minutes before had prepared the crowd by singing a number of stirring spirituals, filled King's silent pause. She knew that King was searching for the right words. She desperately wanted King to share with everyone the dream for America he had shared with her a few days earlier.

"Tell them about the dream, Martin!" she yelled out. New words flooded into King's mind, words that would inspire a nation by giving them a glimpse of his dynamic, God-colored vision. Spirit infused, his words *stuck*: "I have a dream . . ." They were both transcendent and transforming. Even those who considered King to be an ungrateful, unpatriotic pinko commie had to contend with them because King wasn't just sharing an African American dream. He was capturing *the* most deeply American dream. He was speaking for everyone, including my nine-year-old self.

What caused King's speech to *stick* in the minds of billions of people ever after? Why was it so powerful that it led me to read numerous biographies about him, write more than a few graduate school papers on him, and have zillions of conversations about him over the years? Ten years ago, Maria Harmer provided an answer for me.

Maria is my wife's best friend. She's a wonderful spirit and a woman of faith who works in the world of marketing and communications— a topic we've talked about quite a bit over the years because of my interest in the role marketing and communication can play in growing churches. Ever since I took a marketing class a few years after college, I've recognized that we're always marketing, whether we're aware of it or not. We may think marketing is shallow and superficial, but in reality, marketing is merely being intentional and creative with how we share with others our passions. Knowing that I am obsessed with improving how I communicate complex insights and ideas, she gave me a book, saying, "I think you'll like this. It's all the stuff you talk about." It was a book that had become very popular in the communications, marketing, public relations, consulting, and public speaking fields: *Made to Stick* by brothers Chip and Dan Heath.[3]

Sticky Speaking

Made to Stick was a revelation to me because it captured everything I had been trying to grasp ever since I made the decision to look for guidance about preaching in places other than just my seminary classes. The Heaths are fascinating themselves. Chip Heath is a Stanford University Business School professor who focuses on business strategy and organization. His brother, Dan, is an entrepreneur and a senior fellow at Duke University's Center for the Advancement of Social Entrepreneurs. Over the past decade, they have written some of the best books on organizational turnaround, decision-making, and idea development—books I wish all pastors would read. If I could get one book (including the one you're reading) into every preacher's hands, it would be *Made to Stick*. Why is it so impactful?

When we look at the history of preaching, clearly it has emerged as its own field of study, yet its foundations are mostly in the field of rhetoric—the field of persuasion and public debate. Debating is fine in academic and political spheres, where discussions and disagreements require mutually agreed-upon rules of engagement. The problem is that preaching isn't debate. A debate is a battle (from the Old French *debatre*, meaning "of battle") where we try to defeat the other without loss of limb or life. In contrast, preaching is meant to transform, not defeat. Few people are ever truly transformed by a debate, but they can be transformed through a well-crafted sermon—when we share our "dreams."

The Heath brothers' passion is communicating potentially transforming ideas. For example, they've taken a deep dive into understanding why those of the baby boom and Gen X generations can complete this sentence, said by a large-gutted guy in his pajamas sitting on the edge of his bed: "I can't believe I ate the whole . . ." (if you're too young to finish the sentence, ask your parents). They've explored the dynamics underneath the popularity of television advertisements such as GEICO commercials. They've explored why movie lines such as "You can't handle the truth!" and "May the Force be with you" have such resonance. And they explain why "I Have a Dream" shapes our lives fifty-plus years later.

By bringing together insights from business, marketing, and communications, they developed a model for what they call "sticky" communication, a communication in which "your ideas are understood and remembered, and have a lasting impact—they change your audience's opinions or behavior."[4]

Like any good communicator and marketer, they created a fairly simple acronym to capture what makes messages sticky: SUCCESs. This stands for the six basic concepts of "sticky" communication: *simple, unexpected, concrete, credible, emotional,* and *story.* For the rest of the chapter, I will summarize their concepts and apply them to preaching. I hope that after you've finished reading this book, you'll get a copy of theirs, reading it slowly and deeply to apply their insights to your preaching.

Brainy Stickiness

Before we launch into each element of sticky preaching, I want to deviate a bit from the Heaths to talk about why their concepts are so braintastic, why they are in sync with how our brains operate. The more we understand brain structure, the more we grasp why traditional preaching has lost effectiveness and how SUCCESsful preaching can help people listen and hear.

The brain is fascinating to me. It's constructed in ways that make it amazing, efficient, surprising, and frustrating. We don't have one brain; we have five (and I'm simplifying here), which is why it's so easy for us to debate ourselves all the time. The brain is constructed on three levels with two hemispheres. Understanding the levels and hemispheres gives insight into how we can be better preachers. At the base of the brain is the cerebellum, or what some call the "lizard brain." It's the brain that explains why dinosaurs had such huge bodies with brains the size of walnuts. Their brains were almost all cerebellum—the instinctual brain that deals with survival.

The next level is the animal brain. It's the limbic brain that includes the amygdala, hippocampus, and other structures that deal with our emotions, memory, connections with others, and more. The limbic brain regulates our emotions and generates impulsive feelings—wanting to buy that new car or eat that piece of cake, being attracted to this man or that woman. It doesn't speak in words; it speaks in impulses that can feel like screaming voices compelling us to cave in to binge eating, explode in a surge of anger, cry when listening to sad songs, and get excited when receiving a present. It's also the part of the brain, coupled with our lizard brain, that makes it impossible for us to be entirely rational. Why? Because it compels even the most rational person to engage in emotional decision-making. We simply can't get rid of our animal and lizard brains. We can repress them, but they'll deceive us by making us think that these impulses are well-thought-out rational arguments—like dinosaurs dressed in professorial robes, speaking in soothing voices.

Not sure you agree with me? Reflect on that theological "debate" you had with someone from your past. Do you remember feeling your heart beat faster and your face get flushed and having a harder time thinking as the disagreement grew? Of course you were making rational arguments . . . or were you? Your lizard and animal brains weren't dormant. They were involved, trying to "win" the argument so they could feel dominant, thus assuring them that you were safe and secure. For them your argument wasn't about theology. It was about protecting you from threats to your well-constructed belief system that's become part of your identity and core. We do have rational thoughts, but they're always intricately linked with animal and lizard impulses, desires, and instincts. There's no way to separate them from our rational thoughts.

The highest level of the brain is the human brain: the cerebral cortex (the brain cover with all the bumps and fissures) and the prefrontal cortex (the frontal lobes behind our foreheads, which we massage when we're trying to think really hard). This is the conscious brain that we normally think of when we're aware of ourselves and our thinking. This is where rational thinking originates, and the more we develop these parts of the brain through education and training, the stronger our rational, logical thinking becomes—or at least the stronger our belief in rationality and logic becomes.

The lizard, animal, and human brains interact with each other and craft our thinking in ways we're both conscious and unconscious of. This has an impact on preaching, meaning that it is not just a rational exercise. When we preach, we aren't merely preaching to everyone's cerebral and prefrontal cortexes. We're also preaching to their cerebellums and limbic systems. If we ignore that reality, we end up preaching sermons that lead listeners to nap, daydream, look at their phones, or wish they could look at their phones. They'll never invest themselves in our words. They'll never hear us speak about our dreams.

To make things even more complex, our brains have two hemispheres. The right hemisphere is most comfortable with abstract, symbolic, integrative, metaphorical, global, and interpretive thinking. It specializes in the realm of art, music, poetry, literature, and general inductive logic (what we might call "gut" thinking). It's also more "big picture" oriented and emotional than our left brain. The left brain is detail oriented. It's focused on precision, specifics, numbers, order, language, and linear logic. It has a limited emotional range—mostly feelings of frustration and anger when things either get out of control or elude our ability to control them.

The areas of our bodies that each hemisphere controls reflect their structure. The left hemisphere typically controls our right sides. It's the reason most people are right-handed. The right hand is the precision hand responsible for minute operations, such as writing, hammering, painting a table, picking up a coffee cup, turning a doorknob, and anything else that requires precision. The left hand is the general hand that is used more to stabilize and support. What about the population that's left-handed? Typically, their hemispheres are switched, so the precision hemisphere is now on the right side, and the global hemisphere is on the left.

Thus, we have five brains that often struggle to work as one. What does this have to do with the Heath brothers' concept of SUCCESs? When we follow their schema, we become whole brained in our preaching; we intentionally speak to our five different brains:

- *Simplicity* is the first and most crucial element because it integrates the right and left hemispheres. Striving for some level of simplicity allows the global, abstract, and big picture–oriented hemisphere to coordinate with the precision hemisphere's need to grasp ideas in a more linear, logical way.
- Bringing *unexpected* elements into our sermons connects the two hemispheres with our limbic system, which craves surprise and newness (the reason shopping, gambling, video games, and more can become so addictive and why dogs love to go for walks and rides).

- Being *concrete* allows the left and right hemispheres to connect with each other by crafting abstract thought into pragmatic, left-brained language. But it also articulates in ways that the limbic system can embrace because it's rooted in customary experiences.

- *Credibility* takes some explaining, since being credible isn't the same as being factual. For the Heaths, credibility depends on something "feeling" believable because it is based on personal experience, shared experiences, plausibility, or research. Being credible requires appealing to the right and left hemispheres as well as to the human and animal brains.

- I'm sure you get the *emotional* aspect of preaching, although the Heath brothers aren't suggesting that effective, sticky communication is overly sentimental. Emotional preaching evokes laughter, love, anger, sadness, joy, irritation, outrage, helplessness, and a million other feelings. It links the human, animal, and lizard brains with both hemispheres.

- Finally, *story* engages every part of the brain because stories by nature are whole brained and are also transformational.

For the rest of the chapter, let's explore each concept of SUCCESs and discuss how they apply to crafting sermons.

Preach Simply

I want you to think of a short, simple quote, lyric, or saying that transformed you. For example, perhaps this oft quoted phrase attributed to Nelson Mandela (but actually from a novel by Carrie Fisher) is one: "Resentment is like drinking a poison and then waiting for the other person to die."[5] This quote is extremely powerful because it succinctly captures the struggle to forgive. It is almost equivalent to a whole sermon. Shooting for this kind of profound simplicity should be our goal, even if we never consistently reach it.

Being simple is not being simplistic. As the Heaths explain, "If we're to succeed the first step is this: Be simple. Not simple in terms of 'dumbing down' or 'sound bites.' You don't have to speak in monosyllables to be simple. What we mean by 'simple' is finding the core of the idea."[6] The most powerfully sticky ideas come from simple statements that convey a constellation of ideas. One reason I emphasized a model for transformative preaching in chapter 2 (*from-through-to / formation-transformation-reformation*) was to offer a way to simplify the structure of the sermon. A simpler model allows us to communicate in simpler yet more effective and impactful terms.

Simplification also overcomes a significant curse that afflicts all of us pastors. What's the curse? Our education. Simply put, educated people don't think simply. We think complexly because we love complex, abstract, nuanced ideas. Our education creates a disconnect between what we know now and what others can grasp because it also disconnects us from what we used to know and how we thought back when we were laity. The more educated we are about the Bible, theology, the church, and people, the less we remember what our faith and thinking were prior to it, meaning that we also lose sensitivity to where our congregants are in their thinking. A significant advantage nondenominational pastors have on us in preaching (although certainly not in so many other areas) is that many of them didn't go to seminary. They aren't cursed with an education that creates a gulf between them and their listeners.

The Heaths have a simple term for this curse. They call it the *curse of knowledge* (alternatively, the *curse of expertise*). As they say, "Once we know something, we find it hard to imagine what it was like not to know it. Our knowledge has 'cursed' us. And it becomes difficult for us to share our knowledge with others, because we can't readily re-create our listeners' state of mind."[7]

This curse deeply afflicts preaching because we're armed with all sorts of theological and biblical terms, concepts, and insights that others don't have. Yet we unwittingly preach as though they do. How many people in the pews—and especially those unchurched visiting us on a Sunday morning—know what these terms mean: atonement, sanctification, perichoresis, delay of the parousia, soteriology, teleology, Synoptic Gospels, the Gospel, Elohim tradition, priestly tradition, Pentateuch, and so many more? Often pastors complain about how biblically illiterate members of their church are. In many ways, that's a first-world "church" problem. We're lamenting that our church members don't know the Bible as well as we do or that they do not have the desire to know it as well as us. Is that really their problem, or is it that we've spent years and money becoming deeply literate without truly helping them catch up? Perhaps biblical illiteracy isn't the problem because we're the problem: we don't remember what it was like to be them.

This curse can be turned into a blessing when we conceive of our sermons from a lay perspective. When we communicate a complex, profound idea simply and creatively as we might to our formerly uneducated selves, it transforms lives. It creates "aha" or "eureka" moments that inspire. The challenge for preachers is that simplifying is *really hard work*.

There's a reason you and I and everyone else who preaches resist simplifying our ideas, and it is *not* a virtuous stand against dumbing down our sermons. Simplifying a sermon is much harder work than preaching a more abstract, complex sermon. Transforming complexity into simplicity hurts our brains as we rub our foreheads in torment. It causes us to sit for long periods of time while staring out of windows. It's *extremely* frustrating work because we can feel a concept mulling around in our abstract right hemisphere, but our concrete left hemisphere actively resists, telling us to just use the familiar, complex terms we studied so hard to learn. It gets frustrated and irritated at the work because it really doesn't want to translate the abstract into the concrete.

The noted neuroscientist Iain McGilchrist says the problem lies in the fact that the two hemispheres need each other, but the left hemisphere constantly resists the right one. The right one, according to him, is the "master" brain that is responsible for comprehensive thinking, and the left brain is the "emissary" that is responsible for communicating linguistically what the right brain can't. The left brain typically hates translating into words abstract thoughts emanating from the right brain. He says, "Both hemispheres clearly play crucial roles in the experience of each human individual, and I believe both have contributed importantly to our culture. Each needs the other. Nonetheless the relationship between the hemispheres does not appear to be symmetrical, in that the left hemisphere is ultimately dependent on, one might almost say parasitic on, the right, though it seems to have no awareness of this fact. Indeed it is filled with an alarming self-confidence. The ensuing struggle is as uneven as the asymmetrical brain from which it takes its origin."[8]

As I said earlier, the left hemisphere generates few emotions, but frustration is one of them, and when it's frustrated, it becomes like a three-year-old. That frustration you feel when trying to put your deepest thoughts into simpler words is the left hemisphere screaming, "No! No, no, no, no, no!" To convey complex, abstract, profound ideas in simple, logical language is deeply irritating work. It becomes deeply rewarding and fruitful work, though, when it nurtures transforming "aha" moments in others.

So how do we simplify a sermon? It starts with clarifying its core idea. If we can't say what the sermon is about in a relatively short phrase—perhaps fifteen words or fewer—it may be too complex when we put it together. That doesn't mean an idea has to be trite, but it does mean we have to go against our training, which is steeped in the academic, theological realm, one that loves detail, intricacy, nuance, and depth. There's nothing wrong with complexity when speaking to people committed to complex thinking. It's just that the folks sitting in the pews generally aren't those people. Their sophistication, when it comes to religious understanding, typically is not master's degree level or even college level. We have to speak to where they are.

What's our core idea? What significant insight do we passionately want the members of the church to have, and how do we communicate it? Communicating our core idea starts with crafting a summary sentence, like the one we discussed in chapter 2, that captures the heart of our teaching. For example, here's a profound yet short idea for a sermon: *serving God means first aspiring to be inspired by God*. There's a twenty-, thirty-, even forty-five-minute sermon in the development of this sentence. The simplicity of the phrase allows us to streamline the sermon without losing its profundity.

The guidance the Heaths offer us is a formula: "Simple = Core + Compact."[9] Proverbs are an example. What makes them powerful is that they are compact sentences that capture core ideas drawn from experience. And they aren't just biblical. The world is full of religious and cultural proverbs. Many parables, analogies, aphorisms, and more offer us deep, life-giving guidance.

With that, I'll offer two relatively easy ways of simplifying complex ideas for sermons:

1. Identify a complex idea in a recent sermon and pay attention to how you communicated it. Underline the essential elements of the idea. Now rewrite the idea in six words or fewer. You'll get frustrated, irritated, and impatient with the process. Stick

with it, and at the end, you may very well have captured it in a sticky way.

2. Identify a complex idea in a recent sermon and pay attention to how you communicated it. Underline the essential elements of the idea. Now think of a picture, song lyric, or symbol that captures it. Use it as a tool for expressing your idea more simply by getting your left brain to articulate the element you used.

Preach Unexpectedly

Many of my favorite movies have one thing in common, whether I'm thinking about Alfred Hitchcock's *North by Northwest*, M. Night Shyamalan's *The Sixth Sense*, the spy film *The Bourne Identity*, the magician film *Now You See Me*, or Tom Cruise's sci-fi thriller *Edge of Tomorrow*. What makes these stand out is one aspect: you have no idea what's really going on until the end. In some cases, such as *The Sixth Sense*, we have to go back and rewatch it to find all the clues to an ending that we never expected. Their endings come as unexpected surprises.

Humans are hardwired to crave surprise. The Heaths write, "Our brain is designed to be keenly aware of changes. Smart product designers are well aware of this tendency. They make sure that, when products require users to pay attention, something changes. Warning lights blink on and off because we would tune out a light that was constantly on. Old emergency sirens wailed in a two-note pattern, but modern sirens wail in a more complex pattern that's even more attention-grabbing. Car alarms make diabolical use of our change sensitivity."[10]

What makes most sermons boring is that they lack surprise. What we get is completely expected. All pastors follow a pattern in their preaching, and it becomes predictable over time. The most engaging preachers tell stories, offer insights, construct sentences, use their bodies and voices, and develop their sermons in ways that are surprising and unexpected.

The greatest compliment ever paid to me was from a church member who said, "Ever since you became our pastor, I never want to miss a Sunday. I don't want people to tell me what I missed." She wasn't just referring to the sermon. We tried to do something surprising most Sundays. The surprise might be a children's sermon on the Holy Spirit where each person is given a red balloon, is told to blow it up and then release it, and then witnesses one hundred air-propelled red balloons jet every which way throughout the sanctuary. It might be the Advent videos our members created for each Sunday's theme—a stop-motion Lego video on "finding light in the darkness," a video of teens who choreographed a dance to Coldplay's "Trouble" on the theme of "hope versus despair," a family with four boys making a really funny video on "finding joy" that included them having a dance party, and another family doing a whiteboard cartoon video on "patience." Or it may be hosting a '60s- and '70s-themed Sunday where all the performed songs were popular ones from that era.

In preaching I often search for ways to offer something unexpected. I mentioned before an early sermon I did in which I told a story about a new rabbi coming to town and answering his parishioners' questions by dancing as I danced around the sanctuary. Prior to a sermon on learning to live in the present moment, we handed out folded slips of paper taped shut, telling the members not to open them till instructed. In the sermon, I told them that I was going to give them the secret to living a less anxious life—to let the future be the future—and then invited them to unfold their papers and apply the instructions on the paper: "Let it all unfold."

I regularly showed video clips from popular movies to make my points. I sometimes showed videos of music with great lyrics. I sometimes projected pictures and used those to make points. I've had our music director sing a song in the middle of my sermon that illustrated a point. A number of times, I had our associate pastor or a member of the church come forward and share an experience, after which I would talk about what I thought the experience could teach us. I was never hokey in what I did, nor was the intent to "surprise" the members by doing something outlandish. I simply wanted to use the craving we all have for the unexpected to make my sermons sticky.

Making my sermons more surprising had the added effect of making them simpler because these surprising elements took up time. As a result, I've always experienced preaching as fun rather than stressful, because my sermons were creative. Creativity almost always leads to a sense of joy, especially when what we create works. I wasn't stuck in the same old patterns every Sunday. Yes, I did get criticized at times by the older members who didn't always like my "surprises." Then again, the influx of younger visitors and members offset their criticisms, and those older members liked worshipping in a fuller sanctuary.

You're probably thinking to yourself, "I don't have the energy to create something 'unexpected' every week." That's where you're wrong. You don't have to create something fantastically unexpected every week. You can do it subtly. Script out your typical pattern and change it somehow. Here are some simple suggestions:

- *Break a story up.* Tell the beginning of the story at the outset of your sermon. Use that beginning to explore a facet of human struggle. Then finish the story at the end of your sermon to point out how we can be transformed in the face of struggle.
- *Treat your sermon like a children's sermon.* Use an object to tell a lesson. I saw a pastor give a great sermon where she passed out wrapped gift boxes. At a certain point, she asked everyone to

open the boxes. Paper and ribbons went everywhere. The boxes were empty. She said, "I'll bet you think those boxes are empty. They aren't. They're full of God's grace. But we don't have to wrap grace like a present. It's already everywhere."

- *Play a song.* Play a recording of a favorite popular song, and then explore the lyrics with the congregation. At the end, have them sing the refrain.

- *Show a picture.* Hold up or project a picture that captures your sermon or demonstrates something from the sermon.

- *Show a word.* Focus on a particular original Greek or Hebrew word from Scripture. Project or print out the word and let them see it. Then talk about its meaning and relevance to their lives.

The point is that we don't have to be radical to be surprising. We do have to have a bit of courage and a willingness to try something that may fail. But when we introduce something unexpected, it makes what we teach sticky.

Preaching Concretely

People don't like abstractions. They really don't. That doesn't mean they don't like to think or learn new ideas or that they are stupid. It simply means that most people need help in turning theoretical ideas into pragmatic action.

Which of the following two pieces of guidance is easier to integrate into your life?

- When you're experiencing stress and anxiety, you need to calm your mind, still your soul, and let God be in charge.

- When you're experiencing stress and anxiety, try this: Go off by yourself and sit in a chair with your feet on the ground and hands in your lap. Slowly breathe in while thinking, "Let go," and slowly breathe out while thinking, "Let God."

They're both guiding us to do the same thing. The first is more abstract, even if it's less wordy and looks simpler. The second is concrete. As I've stated repeatedly throughout this book, the problem for most of us mainline preachers is that we *love* the abstract. That's one reason we were attracted to seminary. We wanted to go somewhere where it was OK to think about things that are beyond us. We like to explore deep ideas. We like to reflect on realities that seem more real than our reality. Unfortunately, most of our church members—and especially those who have walked away—don't typically have the same passion for our abstractions. They are looking for guidance on how to deal with the challenges, difficulties, and choices of everyday life.

The struggle to be concrete is reflected in the story behind Henri Nouwen's great book *Life of the Beloved*.[11] Nouwen was a fantastic writer who had an amazing ability to articulate our deepest spiritual struggles in engaging ways. At his best, he concretely connected foundational human experiences with deep spiritual yearnings. Fred, a young atheist reporter, interviewed Nouwen for an article in the early 1990s. Out of that interview, they developed a deep friendship. At one point, Fred challenged Nouwen to write a book on faith and spirituality for those who had none. Nouwen accepted the challenge.

The result was one of my favorite books. It wonderfully explores human struggles and desires and a search for transcendence. When Nouwen finished writing the book, he shared it with Fred. He got the following, deflating response, telling him that he had missed the mark: "Long before you start speaking about being the Beloved and becoming the Beloved, you have to respond to some very fundamental questions such as: Who is God? Who am I? Why am I here? How can I give my life meaning? How do I get faith? When you do not help us to answer these questions, your beautiful meditations on being and becoming the Beloved remain dreamlike for us."[12]

In other words, for abstract thinkers like me, Nouwen's book is life-giving water. For Fred, it's too abstract. He wanted something concrete. I feel reassured knowing that even profound writers like Nouwen can miss the intended mark, although he still ended up writing a fabulous book for spiritually yearning Christians.

What makes something concrete? The Heath brothers say, "If you can examine something with your senses, it's concrete. A V8 engine is concrete. 'High performance' is abstract. Most of the time, concreteness boils down to specific people doing specific things. . . . Concrete language helps people, especially novices, understand new concepts. Abstraction is the luxury of the expert. If you've got to teach an idea to a room full of people, and you aren't certain what they know, concreteness is the only safe language."[13]

We don't preach concretely. Nondenominational, evangelical pastors preach much more concretely. Pentecostal pastors preach concretely. Speakers on PBS talk concretely. Even TED talkers speak concretely. We preach abstractly.

So how do we make our sermons more concrete? First, I need to issue a clarification—I am *not* suggesting that our sermons be *only* concrete. We can explore abstract ideas. But we have to do so in ways that then turn the abstract into pragmatic thinking and action. So how do we do it?

First, when creating your sermon, imagine you are delivering it across a dinner table from a teenage kid who keeps asking, "Why?" and "What?" Introduce the abstract idea, but then find a way to make it more teenage tangible. There are so many strategies for this, from using homespun aphorisms ("Gratitude is my purring in God's lap") to giving instructions ("When praying, put your feet on the floor, put your hands in your lap, and breathe four seconds in and six seconds out"). The key is finding a way to connect the theory with a practice.

Second, pay attention to your language while preaching. Are you using Christian jargon? Would what you're saying make sense to someone who hadn't grown up in the church? For example, do you often use the phrase "Christ died for our sins"? What does that mean for someone who isn't really sure about Jesus and who doesn't understand the concept of substitutionary atonement? Can you make it more concrete (I know, I know, it already seems concrete to you, but you also have been *cursed* by your expertise)? What if periodically, when you plan to talk about Jesus dying for our sins, you start by saying, "You know, the whole Jewish faith at the time was based on sacrificing animals as a means to have our sins be forgiven by God. We believe Jesus ended the need for these practices by going willingly to the cross and in effect saying, 'I'm going to take all of your sins—past, present, and future—onto me so that no sacrifices ever need to be made again. Now go out and live in love'"?

Third, feel free to be abstract, but once you are, always ask yourself, "How do I translate this to their left hemisphere or animal brains? How do I use examples, stories, or analogies that make it easier for them to understand?" Again, the key is to engage in a personal exercise of stripping away our accumulated knowledge and expertise by trying to preach to ourselves as we thought before we were cursed with knowledge and expertise. Concrete preaching "sticks" by taking the abstract and making it practical—as much as it can be.

Preach Credibly

Credibility is a difficult concept to define in contemporary life. We are living in an age of false facts, alternative facts, fact-checking, scientific facts, verifiable facts, and fact-free zones. A significant question in our culture is, What's credible and what isn't?

You might believe that credibility is a pretty simple subject—either something is a fact or it isn't. Unfortunately, fact and credibility aren't quite the same thing. Facts tend to be rationally, logically, and empirically true (even if we argue about them). Credibility is where rationality and emotionality meet. In a sermon, credibility is achieved when something makes factual sense while also "feeling" right.

You already see the thorny issue. How can something be credible if it's based on feeling, not only fact? That's the wrong question. The right question is, How can I make what I'm preaching feel logically and emotionally credible? The first question ignores how people really process the world cognitively in the assumption that emotions have nothing to do with credibility. As mentioned above, our brains aren't constructed for purely rational and logical thinking. The more abstract, human, existential, and personal an issue is, the more we will process it with our whole brains rather than just one part. This is a reason politics is so rarely rational. Our animal and lizard brains always want a seat at the table and, if possible, to run the committee of the brain. Thus, recognizing the reality of how brains process ideas and concepts, if our sermon teaching is to stick, it needs to be *humanly* credible. People follow false prophets all the time because they offer what "feels" compellingly credible, despite the potential destructiveness of their preaching. Cult leaders understand this deeply. They know that the people they attract aren't searching for logical answers; they're searching for meaning, safety, and acceptance. They offer these in their messages, albeit in ways that leave their followers vulnerable to abuse. You can rail against that reality all you want. It won't change the fact that people don't just think rationally. They think emotionally. You can either fight against that fact or use it to move people to what you consider a more logical, rational point of view—or a more spiritual, compassionate, serving point of view.

To be homiletically credible means to engage the head *and* the heart in ways that are and feel credible. I believe that as an ethical, moral, called-by-God preacher, you should strive to make sure that what you say is factually and logically true as much as possible. But when it comes to your message, what really matters to those listening is whether what you say has what the Heaths call "internal credibility."[14]

For something to be internally credible, it has to offer details that make it feel true. The most obvious source for offering details is statistics and scientific research, when available. Unfortunately, statistics and studies can be eye glazing and sleep inducing. They're credible but lack emotional surprise and story (which I'll get to in a bit). They can also be manipulated when used without proper context, overgeneralized, or misapplied. Another internally credible source is facts from a shared platform—newspapers, authors, journals, magazines, television shows, and more. The caveat is that our credible source may not be the other person's.

There is one other significant source of internal credibility: *experiential details.* What makes something "feel" credible are the details that draw us in emotionally and physiologically. This connects *credibility* with *story.* How we tell stories makes a difference. Well-told stories feel credible because they have a depth of detail that makes the stories feel "true." We'll talk a bit more about this when we talk about stories. Here it's sufficient to say that the more personalized details we give to a story, the more credible it will feel.

I grew up in an age when pastors often told emotionally disconnected stories. It was typical for them to offer a story that is told something like, "There once was a woman who lived in a very large, far-off city. One day she was sitting on a bench when she saw an amazing sight. Another woman walked by, stopped, and stared at a homeless man on the street. She then went into a shop, bought a sandwich for him, came back, and gave it to him, saying, 'God loves you.' She then continued her walk."

That's an inspiring story, but it only has so-so credibility. Hear it again with details: "Years ago my friend Ann lived in Chicago. She witnessed something that showed her that she could make a big difference in other people's lives through small deeds. She was sitting in Millennial Park when she witnessed another woman act with incredible love. This woman, dressed in a neat, ivory silk blouse; executive skirt; and practical walking shoes strolled by at a hurried pace. Her demeanor practically screamed, 'I'm on my lunch break. I'm really busy. Leave me alone!' Power walking through the park, she suddenly stopped and stared at a homeless man on the street. She immediately turned around and walked into a nearby Cosi restaurant. Ann stared dumbfounded in her direction, perturbed with this woman who was so clearly offended by the homeless man. Still staring at the restaurant door, shaking her head at the woman's heartlessness of using the homeless man's plight to remind her to eat lunch, she watched the woman reemerge with a small paper bag in hand. Walking again with a powerful stride, she made a beeline toward the homeless man. She handed him the bag with a sandwich in it and said loud enough for Ann to hear, 'Sir, I want you to know that God loves you and so do I.' She then continued her walk."

The story is so full of detail that the one listening is sure that it must be true. Yet so often when we tell stories, they lack credibility and tune people out because we make them impersonal and distant. Credible stories are constructed in such a way that they become experiences. They draw us in and make us care. In a similar way, statistics are really only credible when they touch us emotionally. For example, if I was to say that during a recent snowstorm, the snow fell at a rate of three inches per hour, you might care a little. But if I said that the snow fell at a rate of three inches per hour, stranding motorists for up to twenty-four hours on the interstate in subzero temperatures, that would make you care much, much more.

How do we find stories with experiential details? One great source is a new book by a friend of mine, retired presbytery executive and pastor Dan Schomer. *Beyond the Tinsel* is a collection of stories he wrote especially for Christmas Eve services.[15] They are full of wonderful details with surprising endings. But there are many, many books of stories if we're willing to look.

A final source of credibility is our own experiences. I was taught in seminary to never talk about myself in sermons. I discovered, though, that even if people complain about us sharing stories and experiences from our lives, they still appreciate it because they latch onto our experiences as living examples helping them overcome their thorny life issues. There are some rules to this though. First, never make yourself the hero of your story. If we're always the hero, we lose credibility because we make what we have done seem unattainable by mere mortals. Second, add details about how you felt, what you perceived, the humiliating thoughts that went through your head, and what you've struggled with. If the details of the story show our flaws, our doubts, our search for answers, and then an answer, we become much more human and therefore credible. Third, highlight the influence God or others have had on your story. If another person helped us, we should make a big deal about that. If we experienced God, we want to diminish our role in the experience while magnifying God. We thus can use our experiences as a way of helping people find God and transcend their struggles while also showing them that we share their pitfalls and pratfalls.

Preach Emotionally

Perhaps your tradition is a bit different from mine, but Presbyterian preaching is definitely heady. We gravitate toward the intellectual, which is our strength . . . and our weakness. It's fine to speak cognitively and rationally when preaching. Still, humans are driven much more by emotion than we're ever willing to admit. As I discussed above, we are not rational animals with emotions. We are emotional animals with periodic rational lucidity.

The Heath brothers tell us that emotional appeals make what we say matter: "What matters to people? People matter to themselves. It will come as no surprise that one reliable way of making people care is by invoking their self-interest."[16] In other words, the way to make our sermons matter to people is to touch on topics that invoke listeners' self-interest and make the sermon "feel" as though we're talking directly to them by exploring their feelings of shame, anxiety, anger, insecurity, desire, loneliness, confusion, helplessness, joy, love, acceptance, trust, peace, hope, and more.

All good therapists understand this. We cannot move people forward therapeutically until we help them explore their lives emotionally. Good therapists don't encourage their clients to wallow in emotions. They help them become aware of their emotions, their reactions to them, and their behaviors because of them. They also help them understand how their emotions may have led to bad choices and how to use emotionally aware thinking to make better life choices. Similarly, spiritual practices such as mindfulness and contemplation allow us to center in a place and space of calm where we can honestly accept our emotional reactions to life situations and events and then choose how we will respond to them in the future.

I know a preacher such as Joel Osteen elicits shudders in most mainline preachers (an emotional reaction to him as a pastor), and I am clearly not a follower or a fan of his theology, but he is remarkably good at touching people's emotions without ever becoming sappy and sentimental. For example, a typical Joel Osteen sermon *might* sound something like this:

> You may feel that life has pushed you down, but God is always there to pick you up. You may think to yourself, "I never get a break," but you don't need breaks because God's got this for you. Too many of us can see only what we either don't have, haven't gotten, or had taken away from us. But God can show us how much we really do have and have gotten and how much has been given to us. No matter how far down you feel, God is down there with you showing you how far up you can go.

This paragraph is rich in emotion. It acknowledges people's feelings of being down, oppressed, shortchanged, and defeated. It then offers a pathway out of that dark place, one that replaces those negative emotions with hope, faith, gratitude, and perseverance.

We don't have to preach this way to touch people's emotions. There are a billion ways to do that as we integrate multiple intelligences in our own unique ways. What we have to do is to stop thinking that touching people's emotions is somehow manipulative. Everything can be manipulative in the hands of a manipulator. Emotional material is neither more nor less prone to manipulation. Rational thought isn't necessarily free of manipulation. For example, if I were to say, "We can't do that mission because we can't afford it," that's a rational statement. It also can be manipulative because it uses the veneer of rationality to evoke anxiety over possibly losing money. Manipulation always preys on negative emotions, whether it's rational or emotional.

Preach Stories

The final part of the Heath brothers' SUCCESs model is the use of stories. We already talked a bit about this above, and it's the most obvious element for preachers because we have already been trained to tell stories. What we haven't been necessarily trained in is how to tell a story or how to use narrative in ways that really do the work of a sermon for us.

What makes stories so important is that they have the power to embrace all other elements of sticky sermons. A great story in a sermon is simple, has an unexpected ending, is concrete, feels credible, and is emotional. The greatest preachers and speakers have always been storytellers. Why? Because humans love to *listen* to stories. In fact, we do more than listen. We love to *experience* stories, whether they're shared over a dinner table, written in literature, sung to a favorite tune, or experienced through plays and film.

Our lives are personal stories being played out in a much larger drama of life. That's not just a metaphor. We experience our lives as stories. Just notice how we talk with others. When we are deeply engaged with others, we tell them the stories about our lives and listen to their stories. We find connection by sharing stories. One of the best experiences we have is telling a story and hearing our listener say, "I know just what you mean. Let me tell you what happened to me . . ." One of the worst experiences is a similar situation in which someone says to us, "Huh . . . I can't relate. That's not my experience."

Unfortunately, great sermon stories are hard to find. So collecting stories should be a top priority for our preaching. It always has been for me. I've spent my career collecting stories in books; articles; life experiences, both my own and others'; and more. I've often said that I can write a compelling sermon in twenty minutes, but to write an interesting and captivating sermon takes much, much longer, because

PREACHING TO THOSE WALKING AWAY

it may take hours to find a great story to tell within the sermon. A great story tells people more and is more memorable than all the finely crafted sentences we've ever created.

My story search includes clips from movies, television shows, cartoons, music videos, and more as I've become more digital in my preaching. Using clips from movies and television listeners already know and perhaps cherish is even more compelling. I've shown scenes from these and many more films and film series: *Harry Potter, Lord of the Rings, Field of Dreams, Indiana Jones, Mary Poppins, Star Wars, The Sound of Music, Monty Python's Life of Brian*, and *The Blind Side*.

I have certain strategies for storytelling in a sermon. Sometimes I'll begin with an intro, followed by a story that captures an idea, followed by a short elucidation of the idea, followed by another story that explores the idea further, and finally ending with a summary that clarifies the idea. In others I start with a story, stop in the middle and explore an idea, and finish the story with a short summary. In others I might use two or three stories to build the sermon, with each story exploring a separate idea that I then build upon to move toward a transforming conclusion. Finally, in some, if I get a really good story, the story all by itself is the sermon. I frame it with a few sentences at the beginning and the end, and that's it. In the process of all of this, I will have offered simplicity, the unexpected, concreteness, credibility, emotional connection, and . . . story.

Professional storyteller Jack Maguire summarizes the importance of story by saying, "Like our ancestors, we are each personal storytellers to some degree, whether or not we think of ourselves that way. Telling personal tales is an intrinsic part of being human. On a daily basis, as we interact with others, we inevitably wind up talking about our present or past experiences."[17] He goes on to say that we're also personal story *listeners*.[18] We live to listen to stories. It's a significant part of how we learn and grow. A well-crafted sermon story speaks to and transforms all regions of the brain.

Conclusion

My father often told me a story about a sticky sermon that transformed his life. When he was in his early thirties, his pastor, Lockhart Ammerman, preached a sermon about his own struggles to merit God's grace. He shared his struggles and failures and then said something to the effect of, "I've learned that it doesn't matter how often we fall, because when we have a truly deep faith, we can have a *nonchalance* about us. God already forgives us, loves us, and is always there for us. So we don't have to go on living life anxiously. We can live life triumphantly."

My father mentioned that sermon over and over and over again, reflecting on how it made him unafraid to live life fully. When he died in 2015, it was with a sense of that same nonchalance that Rev. Ammerman talked about. My father had lost a fear of death and lived with a sense of joy. Ammerman's sermon was simple, the word *nonchalance* worked because it was unexpected, the point was concrete in its application, it was credible, it was emotional, and it told the story of transforming our anxiety into faith. What could be stickier?

CHAPTER 7

PREACHING SPIRITUALLY

I want you to imagine a scenario. You and your spouse have been arguing seemingly nonstop for the past year. Your nerves are frayed. Your spouse's nerves are frayed. Your children, suffering under the weight of your increasing arguments, aren't sleeping well. They snack constantly on junk food. Their grades are plummeting. A neighbor recently saw your son smoking with a bunch of teens behind a local minimarket. Could have been cigarettes. Could have been pot.

You know you need to do something about your marriage, but you're not sure what to do. You decide to bring up the topic to your spouse. Nervously, fearing this might lead to another door-slamming argument, you start, "Um, I've been doing a lot of thinking lately . . . about us. We don't seem to like each other much, and I'm as much to blame as anyone else. Neither of us is happy. We both know it. I think, maybe . . . what if we decided to see someone who could help us?" Your spouse says, "Yeah, I think it's time." You respond, "Good, I was hoping you would say that. Do you know anyone who has the name of a good marriage *philosopher* we could see?"

What? A philosopher? Why would someone seek out a marriage philosopher rather than a marriage therapist? It's a preposterous question. Certainly philosophers contribute deeply to the transformation of societies and cultures, but why would someone choose a so-called marriage philosopher over a trained marriage therapist who understands human psychology and relationships? You want someone who can sensitively grasp your perspectives, struggles, unhappiness, and situation. You want someone who can offer pragmatic ideas and solutions. You want a therapist.

The scenario I just presented is obviously silly. So here's my corollary question: Why do we consistently insist on offering people *theological* responses to *spiritual issues*? You can say that all issues are theological, but then aren't all marital issues philosophical too? Don't they all involve spouses with different philosophies about relationships, marriages, and life? You still wouldn't send a troubled couple to a marriage *philosopher*, even if they existed. So why do we, in the mainline church, see every issue as *theological* rather than *spiritual*? And why do we treat preaching as a theological exercise rather than a spiritual one?

Preaching Spiritually Rather Than Theologically

As I've said throughout this book (and say here to keep you from feeling the need to defend theology), I'm not against theology. I'm only against the modern dominance of theological thinking over spiritual living that has developed over the centuries because of the dominance of the intellectual over the experiential through the Age of Enlightenment and beyond. Spirituality and theology are deeply intertwined, just as philosophy and psychology are (there are all sorts of psychological philosophies—Freudian, cognitive behavioral, gestalt, Jungian, rational emotive, reality, Rogerian, and so on). But why has there been such a dominance in the modern, mainline church of theology over spirituality? Why can't we hear the clear criticism of those walking away from the church when they say that they are *"spiritual* but not religious"? No one is leaving the church saying, "I'm *theological* but not religious," nor are they saying, "I'm *biblical* but not religious," "I'm *liturgical* but not religious," or "I'm [insert here] but not religious." They're clearly saying "I'm spiritual but not religious" and that we of the church are religious, theological, liturgical, and biblical but not spiritual. They are seeking something more, something personal, something experiential, something pragmatic that connects us with both God and God's higher wisdom for living life.

As I said in the first chapter, I'm incredibly sensitive to this issue, because after thirty-three years as an ordained pastor, I also want to shout out that I'm "spiritual but not religious." Like those walking away, I often have the same reaction they do to typical mainline preaching that's overly theological and "heady" rather than spiritual and "hearty." If our theology isn't connected to a vibrant spirituality and that spirituality isn't pragmatically expressed in our preaching, then people will continue to walk away, and we'll continue shrinking to the point of becoming a quaint group of religious people much like our image of the eighteenth- and nineteenth-century Shakers.

Preaching Platitudinally

What are some of the ways we preach theologically rather than spiritually? One way is what I've called "preaching from the book of platitudes." A platitude is a statement that's so filled with jargon and clichés that we tune it out. We stop thinking, reflecting, and learning. We just endure.

I coined that term after going to a Roman Catholic Good Friday service several years ago. It included the seven traditional Good Friday readings, and after each one, a priest shared a five-minute message. Their messages were all platitudinous. They were jargon-filled, clichéd messages that could easily have been offered twenty-five, fifty, one hundred years ago. I asked my family afterward what they thought, and they all agreed that after the first few messages, they tuned them out and pretty much just endured the rest of the service. Then we facetiously laughed at how the sermons helped us experience Good Friday suffering.

What's an example of a platitudinous message? If we're reading the Matthew account of Jesus in the garden praying, a platitude might be, "Jesus, full of faith, always put the Father first. He's our example. He showed us that it's not our will but God's will that must be done. If we want to be like Jesus, our faith will recognize the primacy and sovereignty of God throughout life." There's nothing to disagree with there. There's also nothing to inspire us. It's theologically correct and spiritually lifeless.

What might a more spiritual reflection sound like? It would focus on the personal struggle inherent in Jesus's experience that also connects with ours:

Put yourself in Jesus's situation. He's struggling. He's hurting. He doesn't want to be arrested, because he knows what's going to happen. He's twisting inside. You can imagine it: "Do I run, or do I do what I'm called to do? I'm afraid! Is this really what Abba wants?" We all have these kinds of struggles at times, although fortunately, it's not about going to the cross. You know what it's like. You want to follow what you think you're called to do, but you're scared. What if it doesn't work out? What if all you get is pain? Jesus gives us an answer: keep praying until we can follow and focus on trusting God in faith as we go forward, despite our fears. This means fighting our impulses to give up, run, hide, or do something to deny or repress. Instead, we continually pray and trust, pray and trust, pray and trust.

Platitudes offer pat, doctrinal answers to deeper questions, doubts, and struggles. They don't engage us in the struggle, and they don't offer pragmatic guidance. They're abstract and general. They tell us what to shoot for but not how to do it, why we do it, what obstacles we'll face along the way, and what personal transformations we'll undergo. Preaching spiritually explores and guides us through all aspects of life's journey, and it helps us navigate pragmatically through the challenges we face.

Preaching Speculatively

Another way we preach theologically rather than spiritually happens when we *speculate too much on the nature* of God, heaven, Jesus, the Spirit, the Trinity, the cross, and more instead of focusing on cultivating the experience of, and relationship with, God. I am *not* advocating that we ignore bigger questions about the nature of God and of life. They're ideal issues to explore in classes, in groups, and even periodically and intentionally through sermons. What I am advocating is that preaching be personal. Too often mainline preaching simply offers information and speculation *about* God rather than guidance on our encounter *with* God.

A great example of preaching speculatively is the way we typically deal with the concept of the Trinity. Today the Trinity is an accepted Christian doctrine, but it didn't start out that way. Early Christians developed the concept of the Trinity because it captured their various experiences of God. They weren't focused on understanding the nature of God. They were expressing how they experienced the fullness of God through personal encounters with each person of God. They weren't as concerned with which person of the Trinity came first or whether each person was a "person" or an "essence." That concern came in later centuries. For them each person was a relationship and an experience.

The early Christians *experienced* God as Abba or Father or Creator—God who is above, below, beyond, before, and after. This is the God of the first chapter of Genesis who is beyond time and space, creates the heavens and the earth, and then declares everything good. They also experienced God as Holy Spirit—as God who is omnipresent, flowing in and through everything, healing people they prayed for, providentially making amazing things happen in their lives, and guiding them through difficulties and decisions. They experienced God as Christ, not only in Jesus, but embodied in each other and all of life.

The writer of the Gospel of John tried to capture in words his experience of Jesus, declaring him to be the animating power of God in creation: "All things came into being through him, and without him not one thing came into being. What has come into being in him was life, and the life was the light of all people" (John 1:3–4). Very few Christians today really embrace the meaning of these words, but John is telling us that God wasn't just incarnate in Jesus. God in Christ is embodied in and through *all* of creation, including us.

Summing up all these experiences, Paul tells us in Ephesians that God is "above all and through all and in all" (4:6). In other words, Father (above), Holy Spirit (through), and Christ (in). John and Paul are both offering early Trinitarian articulations based on their experiences, not final doctrinal statements. So how does this impact preaching? Most pastors today, if they are going to preach on the Trinity, will do so in very speculative terms, talking about the nature of one God and three persons, perhaps talking about perichoresis—how the three are related to one another and how each person of the Trinity is in and within the other two. They might come up with some justification for our being Trinitarian. What's missing in such sermons is the encounter, the experience, the relationship. In a sermon that speaks to our spiritual journey, we might say something like this:

When we yearn for God while looking at the night sky, we are yearning for the Father, Abba, who has made everything, including us, and who loves us more than anything. And as we pray to God to find "me" a job, help "me" with "my" loneliness, or heal "my" mother, we're imploring the Holy Spirit to work through us and the world to respond with grace. Whenever we sense God's presence within us or others, when we're awe-struck by a sunset or shore, mountains or meadows, canyons or cathedrals, we are connecting with and experiencing Christ. The great Quaker writer Thomas Kelly says of him, "Deep within us all there is an amazing inner sanctuary of the soul, a holy place, a Divine Center, a speaking Voice, to which we may continuously return. . . . It is a Light Within which illumines the face of God and casts new shadows and new glories upon the face of men. It is a seed stirring to life if we do not choke it. It is the Shekinah of the soul, the Presence in the midst. Here is the Slumbering Christ, stirring to be awakened, to become the soul we clothe in earthly form and action. And He is within us all."[1] Kelly is speaking of an experience of Christ, not a doctrine.

We have converted not only the Trinity from a spiritual experience to a doctrinal formula; we often take experiences that were originally spiritually relational and transform them theologically into intellectual and abstract concepts.

So what do the spiritual but not religious want? Most yearn for something we *could* offer. They yearn for an immediate, personal connection with God in the here and now—both individually and communally. This is true regardless of wherever people are on the conservative-to-progressive continuum. Those walking away are looking for experiences that connect them with God. If we don't offer them guidance that leads to experience, they will go elsewhere.

Seeking the Experience of God

What makes speaking spiritually to those walking away difficult is that they don't tell us what they really want—because they don't know what they really want. That's why they seek. What's clear, though, is that increasingly, they do not seek in our direction. Many friends and acquaintances feel at some point compelled to confess to me their sin of not going to church and then explain why. It's not really a sin, but they look to me for absolution.

A few years ago, I had a conversation with a friend who, like so many others, was telling me about her spiritual journey and then said flatly, "I think what I'm saying is that my yoga classes have become my church. I feel better physically, mentally, and spiritually afterward, and the people in my class have become my church." What do I say to that? Should I tell her that she should go to a church where she won't feel that sense of body, mind, spirit, and communal connection with God? She was seeking an experience of God and was finding it in yoga.

Another topic that often sets people on a spiritual quest is one that I've done intensive studies on since I was seventeen: near-death experiences. This field has developed a huge following, especially in the past fifteen years. Near-death experience books are among the best selling on Amazon and other online bookstores. Each year more and more people are sharing their experiences rather than keeping them quiet, which is what most did for centuries to avoid the doubt and ridicule they knew they would face from religious and medical skeptics. In spite of my own curiosity, I have spoken or preached about them rarely outside of my own church or spiritual direction, where I'm able to go into depth about them.

Why have I, and others, been so private about this field of study? Because Christians don't know what to do with it. How do you react

216

when someone has an experience of God that doesn't fit traditional Christian teachings? Do you point them to Paul's account of his near-death experience in 2 Corinthians? He writes, "But I will go on to visions and revelations of the Lord. I know a person in Christ who fourteen years ago was caught up to the third heaven—whether in the body or out of the body I do not know; God knows. And I know that such a person—whether in the body or out of the body I do not know; God knows—was caught up into Paradise and heard things that are not to be told, that no mortal is permitted to repeat" (12:1–4). Few Christian preachers turn to Paul to reassure someone who has had such an experience that they are not alone. The results: millions of people find others' accounts of these experiences more valid than our preaching because near-death experiences are just that—experiences. People want teaching and guidance rooted in experience and not just theological reflection and speculation.

It's not just books about near-death experiences that attract those who've walked away. Best-selling authors such as Deepak Chopra, Eckhart Tolle, and Marianne Williamson have offered alternatives to Christian preaching for decades. Some of the best-selling authors who often write on the edge of Christianity and psychology—such as Philip Yancey, Richard Rohr, Henri Nouwen, Rob Bell, and others—attract those on the edge of Christianity. They are speaking to people's experiences and offering guidance on how to navigate them.

I distill Christian spirituality into a simple phrase: "You shall love the Lord your God with all your heart, and with all your soul, and with all your strength, and with all your mind; and your neighbor as yourself" (Luke 10:27). Within this Great Command is everything Christian spirituality teaches. It starts with telling us that the foundation of everything is loving God emotionally (heart), with the depths of our being (soul), with our bodies (strength), and with our thinking (mind). That's the focus: loving God with everything we are. Everything flows out of that. This includes self-care (loving ourselves) as well as other care (loving others through our ministry and mission to them). Too often Christians disconnect from the foundation—falling in love with God—and turn this passage into a treatise on how to love others and ourselves. But falling in love with God is the foundation of all pathways to hearing God, experiencing God, and being transformed by God as well as pathways to helping, healing, and transforming others and the world. The fundamental question for every sermon is whether it is helping people fall in love with God and become conduits for God's love through their personal lives and into the world.

Taking this last step seriously means changing how we evaluate our sermons. Too often we pastors and preachers will ask the questions, Was that a good sermon? Did people like it? Those are the wrong questions. The right questions are, Do people love God a little bit more because of my sermon? Did it transform them just a little bit more? Did it help them experience God's love?

Preaching as the Gateway to God Experiences and Transformation

I've spent a lot of time in this book emphasizing the importance of transformation. Studying the field of spirituality—Christian and otherwise—has taught me that one of the keys to living a meaningful and purposeful life is ongoing learning and transformation. In my near-death experience studies, I have repeatedly encountered a significant message: *our lives on earth are about learning to love.* I don't see that as a conflict with the Christian message. The reality, though, is that love is not automatic in human life. We are born self-indulgently narcissistic, and loving parents cater to our every need—feeding, cleaning, cuddling, entertaining, and protecting. From birth, life is a constant progression from narcissism to compassion. Some make it most of the way. Many stay closer to the narcissistic side. In the Christian tradition, preaching is a primary, prominent tool for transforming people from narcissism to compassion.

The call from God for ongoing transformation isn't just personal. It's historical and cultural, and it explains the great transformation with the advent of Christianity from the prophetic tradition to the apostolic tradition. As I mentioned in chapter 2, prophets were important figures in Israel, but they were rarely transformative. Why? Because their prophecies weren't rooted in relationships. They mostly lived secluded, solitary lives. Hearing God's message, they would reenter society to drop prophetic bombs, often on the king, and then flee back into the wilderness, sometimes running for their lives. They may have been right, but they weren't trusted because their prophecies weren't grounded in deep relationships cultivated with the populace of Israel and Judah, and certainly not with the kings.

The apostles were different. Paul's a great example. Typically, he entered villages and cities composed of mixed cultures, set up his tent-making business, and then went about forming relationships. He talked about Christ and God's presence and love, but those conversations emerged from his relationships with the people of those communities. He first worked on building trust (and periodically failed miserably) and then shared his messages on forging a relationship with God through Christ. Even when he had to drop an explosive, prophetic message, he often couched it in words of tender concern:

> It was to spare you that I did not come again to Corinth. I do not mean to imply that we lord it over your faith; rather, we are workers with you for your joy, because you stand firm in the faith. So I made up my mind not to make you another painful visit. For if I cause you pain, who is there to make me glad

but the one whom I have pained? And I wrote as I did, so that when I came, I might not suffer pain from those who should have made me rejoice; for I am confident about all of you, that my joy would be the joy of all of you. For I wrote you out of much distress and anguish of heart and with many tears, not to cause you pain, but to let you know the abundant love that I have for you. (2 Cor 1:23–2:4)

The early Christians were personal and transformational rather than speculative and abstract. That's how Christianity transformed the world. It started out as a movement transforming people's personal lives, and in the course of that, it changed the world to the point that today, love is regarded by most in Western culture as *the* fundamental value, even if it is not as influential in politics and world events as we might wish. That's quite a change from the often dog-eat-dog values of the ancient Roman Empire in which Christianity grew.

How Do We Preach Spiritually?

If we have any aspirations at all about preaching spiritually, we need to become clear about one thing: spiritual practices aren't spirituality, in the same way that rehearsals and practices aren't performances on a stage, in the arena, on camera, or on the field. I can practice scales, but that doesn't make me a musician. I can practice throwing a football, but that doesn't make me a quarterback. I can practice dancing in front of a mirror, but that doesn't make me a dancer. I say this at the outset because coinciding with the greater acceptance and pursuit of "spirituality" within Christianity over the past twenty years has been an increasing tendency to place the main emphasis on the spiritual *practices* we should engage in so that we can become more "spiritual." The practices we choose to engage in are an essential part of growing spiritually, but just because someone, say, engages in mindful meditation, it does not necessarily mean she will become *spiritually* transformed. The integration of mindfulness techniques into contemporary counseling practice is an example of how a spiritual practice may not nurture a deeper spirituality. Mindfulness and meditation are tremendous tools for helping people overcome grief, trauma, guilt, anxiety, depression, attention deficit disorder, and more. But practicing them doesn't necessarily lead a person to become more "spiritual." Even atheists benefit from the practices.

The focus on practices in recent years can become a form of functionalization, and that's something we all do. In my book *Becoming a Blessed Church*, I talked about how the modern, mainline church has succumbed to *rational functionalism*—the tendency to reduce everything to a set of religious behaviors, beliefs, and bureaucracies that substitute for a live-wire connection with God.[2] I talked about how we adopt agendas rooted in *Robert's Rules of Order* that push God out of our decision-making by requiring us to vote based on what "I" am in favor of. There's no emphasis on prayer, putting aside our will for God's, humility, or discernment nor space given for prayer and listening for God's will. Typical church parliamentary procedure votes using the declaration "All in favor, say yes," which emphasizes voting based on personal desires and interests. It also emphasizes majority rules rather than a prayerful consensus seeking unity. The traditional way of deciding is functional rather than spiritual. A spiritual approach asks people to prayerfully vote based on striving to humbly put aside our interests so that we can seek what God is calling us to do, and it does so by asking people to vote based on prayer, discernment, and the declaration "All who sense this may be God's will for us, say yes." I talked in that book about how we substitute rational theological reflection (although realistically, we often substitute "what I can afford" or "what will preserve what I love") for prayerful engagement.

We can make the same "functional" mistake with spiritual practices. We can substitute prayer techniques, centering techniques, journaling, mindfulness practices, and more for the real focus of them all: *the encounter with and experience of God that lead us to become transformed in and by love.*

I'm *not* saying that practices aren't important. They're just not the focus. They're the tools. They're the exercises we use to learn to live deeper, more expansive lives. We can't grow without practices that support spiritual growth, but the moment a particular way of *being* spiritual becomes the focus, then it loses its power to connect us with God. Thus, any practice that leads to a greater engagement with God is valid. It might be Catholic practices of contemplation, Quaker centering, Baptist Scripture reading, Presbyterian theologizing, Anglican Eucharist, Pentecostal speaking in tongues, Lutheran liturgy, Methodist methods, and more. The key question is whether they lead to greater spiritual growth. The moment we substitute them for spiritual growth, they lose their power. This is the spiritual struggle of all religious movements. Eventually, people love the practices more than they love God.

I talked with a pastor recently as part of my one-on-one work as a spiritual director and clergy coach. He had gone to a retreat where the teacher emphasized the need to journal regularly as a way of growing spiritually. As we talked, he confessed that he hated journaling and felt that it was actually leading him away from connecting with God. It felt like an obligation rather than an invitation to intimacy with God. Add to this the fact that he felt guilty for not liking to journal, which triggered suspicions that he was a failure both as a pastor and as a spiritual person. I reassured him that all these thoughts and feelings meant was that journaling wasn't the right practice for him.

From there we talked about other ways of growing close to God. He talked of his love of nature. So we discussed gazing at, walking in, and appreciating nature as his spiritual practice. The key was that we started with the experience that facilitated intimacy with God rather than starting with an accepted practice. In the process, we integrated the practice of mindfulness and meditation with nature.

So if teaching specific practices isn't supposed to be the focus of helping people grow spiritually, what is? I rely on my training as a spiritual director to answer that question. Three emphases were always the focus of that work: exploring *obstacles and facilitating conditions* for spiritual growth, emphasizing *God as an active presence* in life, and engaging in *disposition formation*.

Obstacles and Facilitating Conditions

I learned early in spiritual direction to focus on *identifying obstacles* that inhibit spiritual growth and exploring the *facilitating conditions* that nurture it. It's a dual focus that translates wonderfully into the realm of preaching. If we are to help people mature spiritually, we first need to identify factors in their lives that get in the way of spiritual growth and transformation. So many issues get in the way of spiritual growth: busyness, work environments, secular pressures and compartmentalization, lack of family support, doubts, questions, childhood teachings, fear, spiritual misconceptions, daily distractions, unrealistic expectations, chronic pain, mental and emotional conditions, despair, dark experiences, ridicule from others, anticipated ridicule from others, Christian denigration of spirituality, functionalization, rationalization, and so much more. Identifying obstacles is the bulk of spiritual direction work, especially early on.

All of this is connected to the process of *from-through-to* that we identified in chapter 2. Spiritual preaching identifies the obstacles that inhibit the process of moving from *formation*, through *transformation*, and to *reformation* while also identifying what facilitates the process. It identifies the struggles people will face if they are to connect with God, navigate the subsequent transformation that comes with that relationship, and positively overcome the discontinuity and confusion that accompany that connection as they embrace new possibilities in their lives. This process relates to both preaching about personal transformation and transforming the world around us.

For example, how can we talk about social justice in a way that takes into account the *from-through-to* process? The reality is that a deep spirituality is never confined to mere personal growth. Anyone who seeks deeper spiritual growth will over time hear the call of God to serve in concrete, active ways. Prayer is never passive. It always leads to action. The dismissive idea that a deeply spiritual person is merely a navel gazer, concerned only with the self, is a myth created by those who are afraid of a deeper encounter with God. Pastors are called to preach about the personal encounter and experience of God *and* are called to preach about social justice—about overcoming racism, bigotry, indifference to poverty, and more. They are called to help people explore their own spiritual poverty *and* to preach Jesus's concern to care for the poor, hungry, naked, imprisoned, marginalized, and oppressed.

Identifying and exploring the personal and cultural obstacles that prevent people from developing a deeper concern for the oppressed and marginalized—and that keep them from engaging in compassionate action—is a crucial part of transformative preaching. We can't just preach prophetically about the need to overcome bigotry. We need to explore the personal psychological and even biological roots of bigotry by looking inward at what's bigoted in ourselves. For instance, we explore how we, as preachers, grew out of our own natural tribal bigotry to be more accepting of those of other races, ethnicities, cultures, gender identities, and religions. We can look deep within to identify the obstacles we had to overcome and then use them to help others identify the obstacles in their lives. To do this we have to make ourselves vulnerable to our own dark sides. It's one thing to tell people prophetically to stop being racist. It's another to join with people apostolically, to share our own struggles (as Paul does over and over in his letters), and to identify the obstacles that we all share. The more we dig into our own motives and struggles, the more we're able to help others transform by then sharing ways of living that facilitate transformation.

So just as we need to identify obstacles, we also need to identify the *facilitating conditions* that enable us to overcome those obstacles. I often tell people that spiritual growth means becoming like water, not lava. What's the difference? Lava, when it flows downhill and confronts an obstacle, hardens and becomes more of an obstacle. Water never stops. It either finds a way around the obstacle, rises above it, or erodes it over time. Preaching about facilitating conditions helps people become like water. They identify what is holding them back, and they learn how to go around, rise above, or erode it.

Spiritual preaching is teaching. We teach listeners how to overcome the struggles they face in their day-to-day lives. This is where teaching spiritual practices in sermons is truly valuable. We can teach a prayer practice as a facilitator for spiritual growth. Many times I've taught the congregation how to be in silent contemplation—how to sit, how to breathe, where to place their hands, what to do with the brain chatter that comes with silence. I've talked about how to practice gratitude, how to discern in a pragmatic way, how to determine what's our voice and what's God (or what's God using our voice), how to use liturgical elements for growth, and more. I've also talked about the spiritual afflictions we have that make us uncaring and how to overcome them through self-reflection and action. I've talked about how to hear God calling us to engage in mission and how to listen for our own unique call to serve God beyond the church. It's not enough to identify obstacles because that alone leaves people stuck with not knowing what else to do. Identifying facilitators offers new possibilities that transform and reform lives.

Whether identifying obstacles or facilitating conditions, we need to go deep, pinpointing the personal, relational, contextual, cultural, societal, national, and global dynamics we all grapple with.

God as an Active Presence

Emphasizing the *experience* of God's presence connects spirituality and theology on a practical level. Theologically, we always emphasize concepts such as God's sovereignty, immanence, omniscience, omnipresence, and more. The challenge for preaching is that these are abstract concepts. Addressing them spiritually makes them concrete and tangible. A significant aspect of spiritual life is growing in awareness, appreciation, and experience of God's presence. A spiritual approach helps us move God out of our heads and into our cognitive, emotional, physical, and relational experiences.

The keyword for preaching on God's presence is *awareness*. Deep spiritual preaching awakens people to the tangible reality of God all around us. It teaches people how to be aware of God in everything. It captures the spirit of an oft quoted portion of the ancient Irish prayer St. Patrick's Breastplate.[3]

Christ be with me, Christ within me,
  Christ behind me, Christ before me,
Christ beside me, Christ to win me,
  Christ to comfort and restore me,
Christ beneath me, Christ above me,
  Christ in quiet, Christ in danger,

Christ in hearts of all that love me,
Christ in the mouth of friend and stranger.

Deep spiritual preaching helps people experience and identify God's presence in encounters with others, such as when someone says something to us and we feel as though God is speaking directly to us through her. Or we hear a lyric in a song that guides us through a crisis. Or we look at a painting or picture that captures our predicament and offers us new insight into it. Or we have an experience that changes our whole perspective in life. Or we undergo painful suffering and trauma that also lead us to let go of our shackles and embark on a new way of living. The deeply spiritual life is one in which people experience God around, in, and through everything. Deep spiritual preaching helps people become aware of and awake to God's presence, especially as it comes through the mundane moments of everyday life. It also helps people realize that God isn't just present in our crises. God is present in every moment, leading us to ongoing transformation and reformation.

As a result of this awakening awareness, deep spiritual preaching *always emphasizes discernment*. It teaches people how to listen deeply and follow God's guidance, especially in times of struggling and suffering. Deep Christian spirituality recognizes that suffering is always a reality on minor and major scales, yet God uses it to transform us.

Ultimately, deep spiritual preaching emphasizes our own agency of choice. It emphasizes how in every moment of life, we face a fundamental choice—*to seek God's way or cling to our own*. So much in life screams at us to *not* choose God. It screams at us to be self-sufficient, independent, uncaring, unkind, and survival-, success-, security-, and self-focused (or at least focused on ourselves and the people we care about). Deep spirituality tells us that in every moment, we can choose between real freedom and biological bondage. Real freedom is the freedom to choose God over everything within us that tells us not to. In those moments, we're faced with the choice between acting out of faith rather than fear; being willing rather than willful or will-less, prayerful rather than prideful, hopeful rather than cynical, open to God rather than sealed off; and following our spiritual nature rather than blindly following our animal one. Deep spiritual preaching helps people make the fundamental choice for God by helping them become awake to God's tangible presence in and through everything.

This brings us back to obstacles and facilitating conditions. Preaching about God's presence and discernment is a matter of identifying what obstructs our awareness and what facilitates greater awareness.

Disposition Formation

Understanding the importance of nurturing spiritual dispositions was fundamental to my spiritual direction training. What is a disposition? It is "the predominant or prevailing tendency of one's spirits; natural mental and emotional outlook or mood; characteristic attitude."[4] A simpler definition is that a spiritual disposition is a natural way we were created by God that allows us to transcend our animal nature and become awake and aware spiritually. We all are created with the ability to embody dispositions such as the fruits of the spirit: "love, joy, peace, patience, kindness, generosity, faithfulness, gentleness, and self-control" (Gal 5:22–23). We aren't limited to these. Other dispositions include prayerfulness, acceptance, discernment, community, and the list goes on. Spiritual dispositions are ways of being that allow us to be transformed moment by moment throughout the mundaneness of daily living.

Spiritual preaching nurtures the development of these dispositions. It calls people to choose to nurture them rather than simply abiding by cultural dispositions, such as indifference, cynicism, conflict, hurry, criticism, self-focus, fearfulness, crudeness, impulsiveness, and others. Disposition formation in preaching integrates what we've discussed earlier by helping people become aware of the obstacles to nurturing spiritual dispositions and identifying what facilitates their growth. It also integrates an awareness of God by emphasizing that as we nurture these dispositions and as they become more actively tangible in our lives, we become more awake and aware of God's presence *everywhere*.

To bring us back to the beginning, spiritual preaching immerses us as preachers in study, but it's study that nurtures the spiritual life by identifying what gets in the way of spiritual growth and what cultivates it. We may do exegetical studies of Scripture, but it serves a deeper purpose of transforming people by nurturing a vibrant awakening to God that leads to a life immersed in loving God, loving ourselves, and loving others with all we have.

As we close, I want to offer an example of how exploring obstacles and facilitating conditions, focusing on awareness of God, and encouraging disposition formation might work in a sermon.

An Example of Spiritual Preaching

The following is an annotated version of a sermon preached in 2015. As you read it, notice how the focus is on the spiritual rather than the speculative.

Breaking Away from Intellectual Idols
Ecclesiastes 1:12–18

This past summer, I had the opportunity to spend vacation time with my dear cousins. We were all so close growing up, but since then, they've all moved to Massachusetts. I'm not sure why. Perhaps it's the ancestral lure of Myles Standish beckoning them to get closer to their Pilgrim roots. Whatever the reason, I don't get to see them much. It's sad, too, because I love spending time with them.

During the visit, I was glad to be part of the twenty-first birthday dinner for a younger cousin. It was a great dinner. It was fun sharing food, stories, laughter, and so much more . . . at least for the first half. As dinner moved toward dessert, everyone began discussing religion, or should I say debating it? This "discussion" has stuck with me ever since. I didn't bring the topic up, but I'm sure some in the family wanted to talk about it in my presence because it was a chance to engage someone committed to the life of faith.

Our discussion/debate reflected a spectrum of religious thoughts, ranging from those like my Episcopalian cousin Betsy, a few who were Catholic, and the rest who were agnostic and atheist. Betsy grew up the daughter of an Episcopal priest. She's heavily involved in her church, having served on its vestry, and her daughters went on many mission trips to Central America and beyond. The Catholic cousins go to Mass almost every Sunday and are involved in their church. The others were, in their minds, recovering religious, having walked away from church because of its growing irrelevance to their lives. *[Here I'm setting up the perspective that many in our culture see the life of faith as irrelevant and as an obstacle to their rational, scientific awakening.]* Their kids weren't raised in the church, so they had little exposure to it.

Then there was me. Having devoted my adult life to religious and spiritual study, I always find it hard to engage in debates with people who haven't. I'm not being snobby. It's simply that eventually I feel as though my nine years of graduate study and my life as a pastor, teacher, writer, and practitioner get dismissed as irrelevant. *[I'm setting up the common experience many of us who commit ourselves to a life of faith have when talking about religion, which is that others see us as being, at best, irrelevant and, at worst, ignorant.]* They argue against religion, but they might as well be having a debate over whether my life has any value.

The conversation eventually vacillated between their views on how wrong and unnecessary religion was and our attempts to prove why it was necessary. For example, at one point, someone offered the age-old trope about how "religion has caused more wars than anything else." *[I offer a commonly adopted, intellectual obstacle many people cite as their closing their minds to a life of deeper faith.]* Whenever I hear someone say that, I always want to put my head in my hands because it's a lazy point of view that lacks deeper insight.

I'm sure someone has offered you this common atheistic wisdom at some point. It's lazy because it falsely assumes that human beings are virtuous, nonviolent, and completely peaceful until religion is introduced. It assumes that when people read Jesus's instructions—"blessed are the peacemakers," "love your enemies," "love others as you would love yourself," and "do unto others as you would have them do unto you"—his words put them into a violent, red-hot rage. It misses the point that you can't *use* religion to start a war; you can only *abuse* religion to start a war. Muslim extremists aren't terrorists because of their religion. They become *religious* terrorists because they see it as a pathway to power, so their pitiful little tribe can rule over everyone else. ISIS and the Taliban aren't pursuing God's will. They're pursuing dominance. *[I'm starting to offer a facilitating condition, which is to separate religious beliefs from common human instinct.]*

Saying that religion causes more wars also discounts the fact that human beings are tribal by nature. Virtually every one of these so-called religious wars has a deeper ethnic or nationalistic source underlying it. *[I am actively disconnecting human tribalism from the spiritual teachings of Christianity.]* For instance, the "troubles" in Northern Ireland are more about conflict between those of Scottish/English and Irish descent than between Protestants and Catholics. There's nothing in either faith to push people to violence, but there is a lot in the natural tribalistic human nature that does. The real issue isn't whether religion causes war. The real question is, How much more warlike and violent might we be if there were no religion? What would restrain us from our tribal nature? *[This is now moving toward spiritual disposition formation by disconnecting a religious perspective from the cultural, human dispositions that lead to violence.]*

The conversation then turned to how unnecessary the church was, how religion was really a problem in much of life, and finally the claim that there is no God and everything in the universe is just random. My cousin Betsy and I became the main defenders of the faith. I offered rational defenses, but what I really wanted to shout was, "I'm right here! You're all telling me to my face that my whole career, my whole life, and my whole pursuit of a deep spiritual connection with God are misguided and false. You're all saying that I've wasted my life!" *[I'm sharing a common struggle we all have when talking about our faith and the fear of being dismissed.]*

Reflecting on our discussion afterward, what stood out to me was how much their intellects got in their way by reducing their awareness to mere rational speculation. *[I'm slowly moving to a new point, which is that being really smart and intellectual can be a significant obstacle to spiritual growth.]* One was a Yale graduate. Another had graduated from Williams College and spent a year at Oxford. Another started his own software company, which has been extremely successful. They thought so rationally and logically about religion and faith that it prevented them from developing a deeper understanding of religion, faith, and life. Their understanding of religion was limited to a teenage or childhood perspective, depending on what age they tuned out religion. To them, rational, logical thinking was the apex of human life, while religion, spirituality, and the pursuit of God were a concrete life preserver that drowned life.

They reflected much of a growing movement of our culture that idolizes rationality, logic, and intelligence so much that they lose the ability to see beyond the *merely* rational, logical, and intelligent. *[Again, I point out a significant obstacle.]* They treat human logic as a religion, never questioning whether there are realms of understanding that go beyond human logic.

PREACHING TO THOSE WALKING AWAY

Don't get me wrong, I certainly believe that intelligence and intellectual pursuits are extremely important for spiritual growth. I have three master's degrees and a PhD. I firmly believe in deep thinking. Some of my degrees are in religion and spirituality. Others are focused on a scientific, rational understanding of human cognition and behavior. Also, being Presbyterian means adhering to an intellectual faith. I certainly can criticize the Presbyterian Church for many things, but a lack of thinking isn't one of them. Presbyterians are among the best biblical scholars, and our approach brings a logical, rational, historical understanding to the Bible. Part of the Presbyterian tradition is believing that we can connect a deep intellectual understanding of the Bible with a deep faith in God. *[This is emphasizing that being intelligent isn't the obstacle, but becoming trapped by our intellects is.]*

The real issue is that deep spiritual awareness requires more than just logic and rational ability. It is important to be rational, logical, and intellectual, but once it becomes a false idol, it kills our ability to understand life more deeply. The fourteenth-century mystic Thomas à Kempis understood this. He said in his classic book *The Imitation of Christ*, "Everyone naturally wishes to have knowledge, but what good is great learning unless it is accompanied by a feeling of deep awe and profound reverence toward God? Indeed, a humble farmer who serves God is better than a proud philosopher, who neglecting himself, contemplates the course of the heavens."[5]

Thomas à Kempis recognized that worshipping intelligence can actually make us ignorant because it keeps us from waking up. Real life is more than just rational thinking and cognitive understanding. It is also about opening up to deeper spiritual aspects of life such as love, awe, faith, presence, and more. *[I begin to emphasize openness to the experience of God as a facilitating condition while also emphasizing how we discover God's presence through experience.]* I don't know why it is, but a lot of really smart people try to reduce life to simplistic formulas. In their deep desire to figure life out, they reduce life to terms that they are confident will rid it of the *discomfort of mystery. [Again, I point to an obstacle.]*

Let me give you another example of how the idolization of intellect can dull our awareness of God. One of our members, Ralph, who's presently a seminary student, had an experience several weeks ago. He gave me permission to share his story. He was at a party and met a man who was very intelligent. Ralph said the guy had thought deeply about many topics. He was the kind of person who continually makes you say, "You're right. You're right. You're right!" Ralph said it was a great conversation.

Eventually, Ralph's wife, Kelli, came up and said, "Honey, we have to go. You have to preach tomorrow morning." The man stepped back dramatically, sighed, and said, "Oh, you're one of those!" Trapping Ralph in a new conversation, he then went on to expound on reasons he didn't believe in religion. A major point in his diatribe was that religious people don't believe in the big bang, which makes them ignorant. Ralph replied, "I believe in the big bang." The man looked at him dismissively and said, "No, you don't!" Ralph said, "Yes, I do." The man said, "You may think you do, but you don't." A deeply religious person believing in the big bang just didn't fit his simplistic formula.

This was a man who had become consumed by his own intellect. He had turned his great intellect into a false idol. He had reduced life to something he could understand by stripping it of depth, complexity, mystery, faith, service, and the experience of God. *[I offer a summary of common obstacles.]*

This man, my cousins, and so many others miss the whole point of religion and faith. The reality is that nobody becomes religious and believes deeply in God because of logic and rationality. I don't mean to say that we God followers aren't logical and rational people. It's just that no one forms a deep faith for logical reasons. We form a deep faith because *we've experienced God. [Now I am strongly emphasizing the facilitator, which is becoming open to experience over intellect and formulas as well as the possibility of experiencing God's presence.]* At some level or another, we have had an experience of God, of the divine, and of the transcendent, and we want to keep experiencing it. *[I'm emphasizing awakening to God's presence.]* We aren't satisfied with mere logic because we know there is more, and that's because we've experienced more.

Frankly, I'm not a pastor because of logic. I'm a pastor because of the accumulation of God experiences I've had in my life. *[I'm now using my experiences to give people permission to experientially awaken to God and overcome their own obstacles.]* People who worship their intelligence are free to dismiss my experiences because they haven't had them, but it's these experiences that led me to seminary. It's these experiences that led me to become a pastor. It's these experiences that led me to get a PhD—all so I could understand my transforming experiences more and help others have them too. *[I'm making it easier for people to accept and validate their own transformative experiences by making them normative.]* It's these experiences that have led me to continue to study, continue to serve, and continue to pursue God. Over time, my experiences have become more vibrant and plentiful, not less.

Betsy was deeply involved in her church because of *her* experiences. Ralph went to seminary because of *his* experiences.

You come to church regularly because of *your* experiences. We worship each Sunday because of *our* experiences. We immerse ourselves in an accumulation of subtle experiences when praying, singing, listening, absorbing the atmosphere, sharing in communion, talking with each other over coffee, and learning. We keep doing it so that we can enhance our experiences. *[Now I'm offering a series of facilitators by emphasizing everything in church that leads to God experiences.]*

Belief in God is very much like falling in love. We don't understand it, we just experience it. Nobody this side of the planet Vulcan falls in love because of logic. Nobody proposes to a partner by saying, "I believe that you are a perfectly adequate person to share my life with and that the biological offspring of our union would make a perfectly suitable contribution to the population of the planet earth." We fall in love because of the experiences we've had with another person that we want to continue having. We stay with the people we love because we love the experience of loving these people. That's what faith in God is like. We experience God, and we want to experience God even more. *[Again, I am emphasizing an awakening to God's presence.]*

We are called into the experience of God not only weekly but daily and moment to moment. Our intellects are part of that experience, but God invites us to so much more. The question is whether we'll say yes to the more. *[I end with an emphasis on discernment rooted in a prayerful disposition that is deeply aware of God's presence.]*

Amen.

Notes

Chapter 1

1 N. Graham Standish, *In God's Presence: Encountering, Experiencing, and Embracing the Holy in Worship* (Lanham, MD: Rowman & Littlefield, 2010).

2 Standish, chap. 2.

3 Alan Kreider, *The Patient Ferment of the Early Church: The Improbable Rise of Christianity in the Roman Empire* (Grand Rapids, MI: Baker Academics, 2016), loc. 337 of 10120, Kindle.

4 Kreider, loc. 4038 of 10120.

5 Kreider, loc. 696 of 10120.

6 James Fallows, "That Weirdo Announcer-Voice Accent: Where It Came from and Why It Went Away," *Atlantic*, June 7, 2015, https://www.theatlantic.com/national/archive/2015/06/that-weirdo-announcer-voice-accent-where-it-came-from-and-why-it-went-away/395141/.

7 For more comprehensive information on the SMOG test, go to "The SMOG Readability Formula, a Simple Measure of Gobbledygook," Readability Formulas, accessed November 29, 2021, https://www.readabilityformulas.com/smog-readability-formula.php.

8 For more on the Flesch-Kincaid readability test, see the entry on Wikipedia: https://en.wikipedia.org/wiki/Flesch%E2%80%93Kincaid_readability_tests.

9 Victor J. Strecher, *Life on Purpose: How Living for What Matters Most Changes Everything* (New York: HarperOne, 2016), loc. 10 of 254, Apple Books.

Chapter 2

1 Walter Brueggemann, *The Prophetic Imagination*, 40th anniversary ed. (Minneapolis: Fortress, 2018).

2 This concept of *formation-transformation-reformation* formed part of the foundation of his concepts and constructs in the field of "formative spirituality," the term he gave for the study of spirituality. He taught that the consonant life is one in which we constantly seek God's directives, which then lead us to always

undergo transformation and reformation. The person most available to God is the one who is always willing to be transformed and reformed.

3 Adrian van Kaam and Susan Muto, *The Power of Appreciation: A New Approach to Personal and Relational Healing* (New York: Crossroad, 1993), 28.

4 Daniel H. Pink, *Drive* (New York: Riverhead), loc. 20 of 180, Apple Books.

5 Pink, loc. 69 of 180.

6 Pink, loc. 92 of 180.

7 Pink, loc. 136 of 180.

Chapter 3

1 Ken Wilber, *The Marriage of Sense and Soul: Integrating Science and Religion* (New York: Random House, 2011).

2 Wilber, 99.

3 Wilber, 18.

4 *The Constitution of the Presbyterian Church (U.S.A.) Part II Book of Order 2019–2021* (Louisville, KY: Office of the General Assembly, 2019), F-1.0304.

5 Chris Columbus, dir., *Harry Potter and the Sorcerer's Stone* (Burbank, CA: Warner Brothers, 2001).

Chapter 4

1 William Strauss and Neil Howe, *Generations: The History of America's Future, 1584 to 2069* (New York: Quill, 1991).

2 William Strauss and Neil Howe, *The Fourth Turning: An American Prophecy: What the Cycles of History Tell Us about America's Next Rendezvous with Destiny* (New York: Penguin Random House, 1997).

3 Strauss and Howe, 277–78.

4 Socrates, "Quotable Quote," Goodreads.com, https://www.goodreads.com/quotes/63219-the-children-now-love-luxury-they-have-bad-manners-contempt.

5 Strauss and Howe, *Generations*, 92–96.

6 Strauss and Howe, 74.

7 Setting a date of 2001 is my own choice, since Strauss and Howe did not set an end date. I chose this date simply because it is the year 9/11 occurred, which became the first of many crises experienced by Generation Z throughout their childhood and seems to be a clear marker between them and millennials.

8 Josh Packard and Ashleigh Hope, *Church Refugees: Sociologists Reveal Why People Are Done with Church but Not Their Faith* (Loveland, CO: Group Publishing), loc. 83 of 144, Kindle.

9 Packard and Hope, loc. 82 of 144.

10 Josh Packard, *Meaning Making: 8 Values That Drive America's Newest Generations* (Bloomington, MN: Springside Research Institute, 2020), 8.

11 Packard, 34.

12 Packard, 43.

13 Packard, 79.

14 Michelle Ye Hee Lee, "Gen Z, Millennial Voters Embrace Activism and Voting, as Youth Turnout Surges ahead of Election Day," *Washington Post*, October 29, 2020.

15 Packard, *Meaning Making*, 92.

16 Packard, 107–8.

17 Diana L. Howles, "The TED Talk 'C' Principles: 5 Tips for Your Own Presentations," *Training Magazine* website, https://trainingmag.com/the-ted-talk-c -principles.

18 Anthony de Mello, *The Song of the Bird* (New York: Doubleday, 1984), 153.

Chapter 5

1 Howard E. Gardner, *Multiple Intelligences: New Horizons in Theory and Practice* (New York: Basic Books, 2006), loc. 18 of 275, Apple Books, https://books .apple.com/us/book/multiple-intelligences/id1210027697.

2 Howard Gardner, *Frames of Mind: The Theory of Multiple Intelligences* (New York: Basic Books, 1983).

3 Howard Gardner, *Intelligence Reframed: Multiple Intelligences for the 21st Century* (New York: Basic Books, 1999).

4 Gardner, *Multiple Intelligences*, loc. 18 of 393.

5 Gardner, loc. 20–41 of 393.

6 Samaritan Counseling-Guidance-Consulting, "Third Week of Advent Clergy Worship: 'Pray. Breathe. Laugh,'" YouTube video, December 12, 2020, https:// www.youtube.com/watch?v=SM6eVdBw2Us.

7 Gardner, *Multiple Intelligences*, loc. 27 of 393.

8 Gardner, loc. 34–35 of 393.

9 Gardner, loc. 37 of 393.

10 Gardner, loc. 40 of 393.

Chapter 6

1 Martin Luther King Jr., "I Have a Dream," August 28, 1963, Washington, DC, American Rhetoric, https://www.americanrhetoric.com/speeches/mlk ihaveadream.htm.

2 Tim Harford, "Martin Luther King Jr.; the Jewelry Genius; and the Art of Public Speaking," in *Cautionary Tales*, podcast, February 26, 2021, https:// playlist.megaphone.fm/?p=CAD6536215675.

3 Chip Heath and Dan Heath, *Made to Stick: Why Some Ideas Survive and Others Die* (New York: Random House, 2007), Kindle.

4   Heath and Heath, loc. 130–131 of 5194.

5   "Resentment Is like Taking Poison and Waiting for the Other Person to Die," Quote Investigator, https://quoteinvestigator.com/2017/08/19/resentment/.

6   Heath and Heath, *Made to Stick*, loc. 450 of 5194.

7   Heath and Heath, loc. 324 of 5194.

8   Iain McGilchrist, *The Master and His Emissary: The Divided Brain and the Making of the Western World* (New Haven, CT: Yale University Press, 2019), loc. 309 of 17309, Kindle.

9   Heath and Heath, *Made to Stick*, loc. 738 of 5194.

10 Heath and Heath, loc. 1041 of 5194.

11 Henri J. M. Nouwen, *Life of the Beloved: Spiritual Living in a Secular World* (New York: Crossroad, 2014).

12 Nouwen, 140.

13 Heath and Heath, *Made to Stick*, loc. 1680 of 5194.

14 Heath and Heath, loc. 2209–2390 of 5195.

15 Dan Schomer, *Beyond the Tinsel: Short Stories for Christmas Eve* (Benton, AR: Resource Publications, 2020).

16 Heath and Heath, *Made to Stick*, loc. 2885 of 5194.

17 Jack Maguire, *The Power of Personal Storytelling: Spinning Tales to Connect with Others* (New York: Jeremy P. Tarcher, 1998), xiv.

18 Maguire, 5.

Chapter 7

1   Thomas Kelley, *A Testament of Devotion* (San Francisco: HarperSanFrancisco, 1992), 3.

2   N. Graham Standish, *Becoming a Blessed Church: Forming a Church of Spiritual Purpose, Presence, and Power*, rev. ed. (New York: Rowman & Littlefield, 2016), chap. 1, Kindle.

3   No one is entirely sure where this prayer came from other than that it originates from the Irish Celtic tradition rooted in the teachings and mission of Saint Patrick. It is often attributed to him, and he may very well have written it in a form that was subsequently edited and shaped over the centuries.

4   Dictionary.com, s.v. "disposition," accessed October 8, 2021, https://www.dictionary.com/browse/disposition.

5   Thomas à Kempis, *The Imitation of Christ*, trans. William C. Creasy (Notre Dame, IN: Ave Maria, 1989), 31.